BATMAN

CHARACTER ENCYCLOPEDIA

WRITTEN BY **MATTHEW K. MANNING**

BATMAN CREATED BY **BOB KANE** WITH **BILL FINGER**

INTRODUCTION

Delve into Batman's world and meet noble Super Heroes, terrifying super-villains, and everyone in between. Discover honourable vigilantes, deadly assassins, heroes gone bad, humans that transform into animals, honest cops and time-travelling warlords. Who is your favourite? Who wears the best costume? And who has the strangest superpower? Turn the page and find out!

Contents

Every character in this book has his or her own role to play. Noble heroes use their powers and weapons to fight for justice. The Dark Knight's allies might not have superpowers, but they help out when they can. Neutral characters have been both friend and foe to Batman. Whose side are they on now? And, of course, the rogues — dangerous villains who try to thwart the Dark Knight at every turn. To find a character at superhuman speed, use the index at the back of the book.

BATMAN

HERO

VITAL STATS

Real Name: Bruce Wayne
Occupation: Hero, crime fighter
Height: 1.87 m
Weight: 95 kg
Base: Gotham City
Allies: The Batman Family, the Justice League, Batman, Inc.
Foes: Arkham Rogues, Rā's al Ghūl, the Penguin

POWERS AND ABILITIES

Martial artist; near-genius intellect; skilled detective and gymnast; armoured suit and Utility Belt equipped with myriad offensive and defensive devices.

BEWARE THE BAT
Bruce Wayne adopted the image of a bat in order to strike fear into the hearts of criminals everywhere. This intimidating persona was inspired by Bruce's own childhood encounter with the bats living below Wayne Manor.

After his parents were gunned down before his eyes in a senseless act of violence when he was just a young boy, Bruce Wayne dedicated his entire life to protecting the citizens of Gotham City. To that end, he trained his body and mind to near physical perfection and used the Wayne family fortune to create a hi-tech arsenal of unique weapons and vehicles.

Arm gauntlets adorned with scallops that can be used as weapons

Cape helps instill fear in criminals and protects him from gunfire and flames

Bat-symbol has helped make him notorious

Armoured Batsuit has reinforced plates at the knees

"Father, I shall become a bat."

BRUCE WAYNE

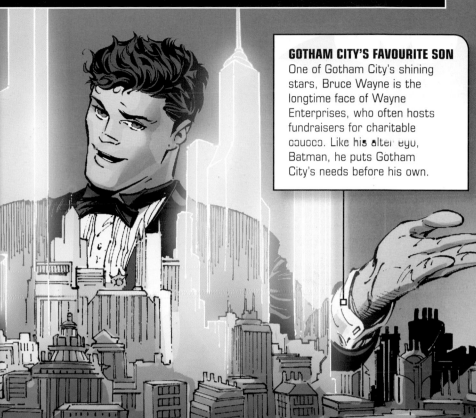

VITAL STATS

Full Name: Bruce Wayne

Occupation: Former head of Wayne Enterprises

Height: 1.87 m

Weight: 95 kg

Base: Gotham City

Allies: The Batman Family, the Justice League, Batman, Inc.

Foes: Arkham Rogues, Rā's al Ghūl, the Penguin

POWERS AND ABILITIES

Near-genius intellect; incredible social skills; carefully constructed public persona conceals alter ego; enormous resources at his disposal due to contacts at Wayne Enterprises.

GOTHAM CITY'S FAVOURITE SON

One of Gotham City's shining stars, Bruce Wayne is the longtime face of Wayne Enterprises, who often hosts fundraisers for charitable causes. Like his alter ego, Batman, he puts Gotham City's needs before his own.

Bruce Wayne became the Batman, fighting to protect Gotham City. However, when he returned to his hometown from travelling and training abroad, he realised the need to create a public persona that would distance him from his nocturnal activities. Bruce became involved in Wayne Enterprises, and built a reputation for himself as a careless bachelor.

"A better, brighter Gotham is just one dream away."

Hides in plain sight as public figure

Often dresses formally for social engagements

Can change into Batsuit at lightning speed

Tuxedo from his expensive wardrobe

ROBIN

HERO

VITAL STATS

Real Name: Damian Wayne

Occupation: Hero, adventurer

Height: 1.37 m

Weight: 38 kg

Base: Gotham City

Allies: Batman, the Batman Family, Batman, Inc., Goliath

Foes: Rās al Ghūl, the League of Assassins, NoBody

POWERS AND ABILITIES

Martial artist; skilled detective and gymnast; adept assassin; impressive intellect; as Robin, employs armoured suit equipped with a myriad of offensive and defensive devices; protected by a Man-Bat named Goliath; briefly possessed Superman-like powers.

FATHER AND SON

Batman has mentored several Robins, but none have been his own flesh and blood until Damian. Despite his stubborn personality, Damian holds a special place in the Dark Knight's carefully guarded heart.

The result of a romance between Batman and the corrupt Talia al Ghūl, Damian Wayne was grown in a lab. Once he was brought into the world, Talia trained Damian in the deadly ways of the League of Assassins before allowing Batman to meet his son. Damian soon abandoned his mother's violent ways and joined his father as his new partner, Robin.

"I'm going out, Father. Gotham needs me."

Trained in martial arts

Utility Belt with smoke pellets and tear gas

Gauntlets similar to Batman's

GRAYSON

VITAL STATS

Full Name: Richard "Dick" Grayson

Occupation: Agent of Spyral, gymnastics teacher

Height: 1.78 m

Weight: 79 kg

Base: Saint Hadrian's Finishing School for Girls, England

Allies: Batman, the Batman Family, Helena Bertinelli, Starfire

Foes: The Joker, Prankster, Paragon, Tony Zucco

POWERS AND ABILITIES

Highly skilled acrobat; natural athlete; martial artist; extremely intelligent; trained by Batman; can alter appearance via identity protection implants.

LIGHTS OUT AT MIDNIGHT

Grayson's adventures with Spyral have put him in direct opposition with the vigilante known as the Midnighter on several occasions. What Midnighter doesn't know is that Grayson is secretly a double agent for Batman.

Equipped with mind-influencing "hypnos"

Favourite weapons are escrima sticks

Belt equipped with variety of hi-tech gadgets

Soon after young trapeze artist Dick Grayson watched his parents fall to their deaths, he embarked on a new chapter in his life as Bruce Wayne's adopted son and Batman's partner, Robin. After growing into a Super Hero in his own right — Nightwing — Dick later retired that name after a near-death experience, and went to work at the spy agency Spyral as Agent 37.

"We've got some lives to save."

RED HOOD

VITAL STATS

Real Name: Jason Todd

Occupation: Vigilante for hire

Height: 1.83 m

Weight: 82 kg

Base: Los Angeles, California

Allies: The Outlaws, the Batman Family, Talia al Ghūl, the League of Assassins

Foes: The Joker, Rā's al Ghūl, the Untitled

POWERS AND ABILITIES

Martial artist; skilled detective and gymnast; adept assassin; impressive intellect; trained by Batman; armoured suit equipped with offensive and defensive devices.

OUTLAW BY CHOICE

Jason Todd was given a second lease of life thanks to Talia al Ghūl and the healing properties of the Lazarus Pit. He transitioned from Robin to the Red Hood, and teamed up with other like-minded heroes.

Jason Todd was discovered by the Joker at an early age. The Joker had Jason's father arrested and faked his mother's death, manoeuvring the boy into position to become Batman's newest Robin. Now in a position to destabilise the Batman family, the Joker killed Jason, not knowing that the young man would later return to life as the Red Hood.

Wears hi-tech protective helmet

Armoured suit equipped with myriad devices

Red bat symbol on his costume

"I don't work for just anyone."

RED ROBIN

VITAL STATS

Real Name: Timothy Drake

Occupation: Hero

Height: 1.68 m

Weight: 59 kg

Base: New York City

Allies: The Teen Titans, Batman, the Batman Family, Spoiler

Foes: The Penguin, the Mad Hatter, the Joker

POWERS AND ABILITIES

Martial artist; skilled detective and gymnast; impressive intellect; excellent computer hacker; protective Spider suit equipped with myriad offensive and defensive devices; natural born leader.

A DIFFERENT DRUMMER

As the third person to bear the name Robin, Tim Drake decided to set himself apart from the crowd and opted for the title Red Robin instead. After serving as Batman's partner for a time, he soon formed his own team, the Teen Titans.

A gifted gymnast and scholar, high school student Tim Drake wanted nothing more than to fight crime with the Dark Knight. To that end, he used his computer hacking skills to steal the Penguin's fortune. The Penguin retaliated against Tim's family, forcing Batman to place them in protective custody. Tim stayed in Gotham City and became Batman's partner, Red Robin.

"I want to apply for the job."

Red Robin's role as the leader of the Teen Titans has placed him in many life-and-death situations, including facing the villain known as Grymm.

BATGIRL

VITAL STATS

Real Name: Barbara Gordon
Occupation: Hero, graduate student
Height: 1.80 m
Weight: 61 kg
Base: Burnside, Gotham City
Allies: The Birds of Prey, the Batman Family, James Gordon
Foes: The Joker, James Gordon, Jr, Knightfall, Velvet Tiger

POWERS AND ABILITIES

Expert martial artist and gymnast; intelligent and excellent strategist; natural leader; athletic and agile; uses compactible Batcycle; trained by Batman.

PACKING A PUNCH

Batgirl has worn several costumes over the years. She adopted her second official uniform when returning to crime fighting after a temporary hiatus. This costume was highly armoured and utilised all of Batman's technology.

The daughter of police commissioner James Gordon, Barbara Gordon idolised Batman from a young age. One day, at police headquarters, Barbara adopted a police-developed Batsuit to protect her brother from an escaping criminal. After Batman complimented her on her actions, she realised her true calling and donned a mask and cape as Batgirl.

"Shut up and hug, tough girl."

Can remember with expert precision

Designed her own protective costume

Smartphone to use social media to her advantage

Fully stocked Utility Belt

BATWOMAN

VITAL STATS

Real Name: Katherine (Kate) Kane

Occupation: Hero, socialite

Height: .80 m

Weight: 64 kg

Base: Gotham City

Allies: Hawkfire, Batman, the Batman Family, the Unknowns

Foes: Nocturna, Ceto, Wolf Spider, Mr Bones

POWERS AND ABILITIES

Martial artist; skilled detective and gymnast; highly trained soldier studied under elite operatives known as the Murder of Crows.

ESTRANGED FAMILY

Unlike Batgirl or Robin, Batwoman doesn't operate with Batman's seal of approval. The two clashed when Batwoman's then employers, the Department of Extranormal Operations (D.E.O.), ordered her to find out the Dark Knight's secret identity.

Bruce Wayne's cousin Kate Kane lived a happy life, until her mother was killed. Kate was raised by her father, Colonel Jacob Kane, whose military connections enabled her to train with some of the world's finest fighters. Kate struggled to find her direction in life until an encounter with Batman inspired her to fight crime in her own unique style as Batwoman.

*"I will **soldier on**."*

Wears long-haired wig to mask identity

Arm gauntlets can fire grappling line

Protective suit equipped with myriad devices

Utility Belt houses array of useful tools

HERO

VITAL STATS

Real Name: Stephanie Brown

Occupation: Hero, student

Height: 1.65 m

Weight: 50 kg

Base: Gotham City

Allies: Red Robin, Bluebird, Catwoman, Batman

Foes: Cluemaster, Hush, Lincoln March

POWERS AND ABILITIES

Skilled motorcyclist; smart mind and able to think quickly on her feet; skilled gymnast and fighter; protective suit equipped with offensive and defensive devices.

SPOILER ALERT

As a kid, Stephanie Brown liked to push the envelope and attempt extremely difficult bike stunts. So it wasn't much different for her to risk life and limb when she adopted the vigilante role of the Spoiler.

Stephanie Brown's life changed drastically when she interrupted her father's "puzzle night" with his friends, only to learn he was the super-villain known as Cluemaster. On the run from her parents, Stephanie soon discovered that her father was behind a scheme to destroy Batman. She fought against him, and adopted the identity of the costumed Super Hero called the Spoiler.

"No, Dad. You're done. I'm just getting started."

After the Cluemaster was defeated, Spoiler still wanted to pursue a Super Hero lifestyle, and pleaded with Catwoman to train her.

AZRAEL

VITAL STATS

Real Name: Michael Washington Lane
Occupation: Hero
Height: 1.88 m
Weight: 95 kg
Base: Gotham City
Allies: Batman, the Batman Family, the Order of Purity, Batman, Inc.
Foes: Rā's al Ghūl, Leviathan, Dr Hurt

POWERS AND ABILITIES

Advanced military and police training; wears protective mystical armour; excellent hand-to-hand combatant; skilled swordsman; wields the magical Sword of Sin and Sword of Salvation.

LIFE OF SORROW

Azrael wears the Suit of Sorrows, an ancient suit of armour that Batman once wore. Azrael was once deputised into Batman, Inc., where he lent Batman his armour to wear in battle against the forces of the terrorist agency Leviathan.

Michael Lane was a former college athlete and a Marine who joined the Gotham City Police Department, but was later dismissed. However, Lane joined a secret programme between the military and the G.C.P.D. to create a Batman replacement. Later, Lane was approached by a covert organisation called the Order of Purity, to be their vigilante, Azrael.

Suit of Sorrows armour is cursed

Mystical Sword of Salvation brings the truth to light

Costume reflects extreme religious mindset

"I am God's vengeance... his angel of death."

ALFRED PENNYWORTH

VITAL STATS

Full Name: Alfred Pennyworth
Occupation: Bruce Wayne's butler
Height: 1.83 m
Weight: 72.5 kg
Base: Gotham City
Allies: Batman, the Batman Family, Julia Pennyworth
Foes: Arkham Rogues, Hush

POWERS AND ABILITIES

Skilled surgeon; military combat training; expert actor; computer expert; valued confidant.

A STEADY HAND

There is far more to Alfred's responsibilities than cooking and cleaning for billionaire Bruce Wayne. With full knowledge of Batman's identity, Alfred has saved Bruce's life on many occasions, putting his surgery skills to good use.

As loyal butler to Thomas and Martha Wayne, Alfred Pennyworth did his best to raise their son Bruce after their tragic deaths. Alfred stood by his young master's side, helping him build his career as Batman. While he often wishes Bruce would retire from crime fighting, Alfred nevertheless feels honoured to play a role in Batman's mission.

"...I'll always be there to patch you up."

Dubbed Penny-One during radio transmissions, Alfred often works at the Batcomputer, feeding Batman information when he is in the field.

JULIA PENNYWORTH

ALLY

VITAL STATS

Full Name: Julia Pennyworth

Occupation: Batman task force strategist, former SRR agent

Height: 1.73 m

Weight: 58.5 kg

Base: Gotham City

Allies: Batman, James Gordon, Alfred Pennyworth, G.C.P.D.

Foes: Shen Fang, Hush, the Joker

POWERS AND ABILITIES

Highly trained special agent; expert marksman; computer expert; efficient spy and strategist; has access to Batman's crime files and technology.

IN FOR A PENNY...

Julia began helping Batman from the Batcave as Penny-Two after Alfred was injured by Hush. After Batman's assumed "death", she began working as part of the G.C.P.D.'s Batman task force as Julia Perry.

An agent for the British Special Reconnaissance Regiment, Julia Pennyworth first crossed paths with Batman in Hong Kong when he was investigating Carmine Falcone and Shen Fang. Fang stabbed Julia, badly injuring her. Learning that Julia was Alfred's daughter, Batman brought her to Wayne Manor, where she discovered his double life and reconciled with her father, Alfred.

"Turn on the lights down here and show Jim his Batmobile."

It didn't take Julia long to figure out the Batcomputer. She usually assists from the Batcave, but has occasionally ventured out into the field.

BATWING

VITAL STATS

Real Name: Lucas "Luke" Fox

Occupation: Hero, mixed martial arts fighter

Height: 1.75 m

Weight: 77 kg

Base: Gotham City

Allies: Batman, Lucius Fox, the Batman Family, Batman, Inc.

Foes: Lady Vic, Ratcatcher, Charlie Caligula, Menace

POWERS AND ABILITIES

Talented martial arts fighter; brilliant designer and engineer; quick witted; suit allows for hi-tech weaponry and defence systems, flight and limited invisibility; near unlimited access to Wayne Enterprises technology.

WINGING IT

One of Batwing's first missions had him partner with Batman to face the Marabunta, an ant-like colony of villains employed by the criminal Charlie Caligula. Batwing defeated the organisation's sects in Africa and Gotham City.

When Batman formed his crime-fighting organisation, Batman, Inc., he hand-picked worthy individuals to join the team. He chose Luke, son of his longtime friend — and Wayne Enterprises CEO — Lucius Fox, to become the armoured hero Batwing. While his secret Batwing career has caused family problems for Luke, he has embraced life as a Super Hero.

"It's all part of my job."

Bat-symbol can project bursts of brilliant light

Built-in Utility Belt to store small devices

Helmet equipped with "Detective Vision"

Bulletproof armour protects and seals underwater

Gauntlets can fire grappling line

BLUEBIRD

VITAL STATS

Real Name: Harper Row
Occupation: Hero, student
Height: 1.65 m
Weight: 51 kg
Base: Gotham City
Allies: Batman, Red Robin, the Batman Family, Cullen Row
Foes: The Mad Hatter, the Joker, Lincoln March

POWERS AND ABILITIES

Electronics expert; great at fixing things; protective suit equipped with myriad offensive and defensive devices; uses taser rifle.

NO KILLING A MOCKINGBIRD

After repeatedly proving her worth to Batman, Harper Row began to fight by Red Robin's side. She eventually developed her own identity as Bluebird to battle the Mad Hatter, and became Batman's newest ally.

The daughter of a deadbeat father, Harper Row was forced to take on responsibilities at an early age and practically raised her brother Cullen. As a teenager with a talent for electronics, she and her brother were rescued by the Batman one night. Inspired by the hero, Harper hacked into his network and helped in a battle with Tiger Shark.

"Batman doesn't get to die."

Cut hair to take a stand against brother's bullies

Suit has anti-nanotechnology barrier

Belt contains smoke capsules and Batarangs

TALON

VITAL STATS

Real Name: Calvin Rose

Occupation: Hero

Height: 1.78 m

Weight: 79 kg

Base: Gotham City

Allies: Batman, Batman, Inc., Strix, Casey Washington

Foes: The Court of Owls, Bane, Lord Death Man, Sebastian Clark

POWERS AND ABILITIES

Expert escape artist; adept in several fighting styles and knife-throwing; knowledge of electronics, specifically security systems; expert assassin, despite now practising non-lethal crime fighting.

OWL VS. BAT

At first Batman did not approve of Talon's crusade against the Court of Owls, fearing innocent lives may be in jeopardy. However, he soon saw Talon's true heroism, and recruited him into Batman, Inc.

At eight years old, Calvin Rose was locked and abandoned in a dog kennel by his father. After three nights, he managed to break out, and was discovered by an escape artist who worked at Haly's Circus. Calvin trained and became the man's successor, and was then recruited by the Court of Owls as a Talon assassin. But he escaped that world too, in favour of the life of a hero.

Armour gifted to him by the Court of Owls

Belt equipped with items like lock picks

Gauntlets can fire grappling line and darts

"I'm never running away again."

HAWKFIRE

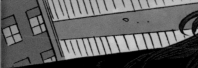

VITAL STATS

Real Name: Bette Kane
Occupation: Student, crime fighter
Height: 1.68 m
Weight: 54 kg
Base: Gotham City
Allies: Batwoman, Jacob Kane
Foes: The Hook, Mr Freeze, Bane

POWERS AND ABILITIES

Martial artist; skilled detective and gymnast; trained by Batwoman and Jacob Kane; studied under elite operatives known as the Murder of Crows; wing pack allows her to fly.

A DYNAMIC DUO?

Hawkfire is the optimistic Robin to Batwoman's more practical Batman. Full of life and hope, with more than a little skill of her own, Hawkfire has proven herself as a true crime fighter, despite Batwoman's concerns.

Bette Kane's desire to be a Super Hero was long held. Originally operating as the crime-fighting heroine Flamebird, Bette learnt that her cousin Kate Kane was moonlighting as Batwoman. Kate took her cousin under her wing and Bette adopted the identity of Hawkfire. Operating as Batwoman's sometime partner, Bette is helped out by her uncle, Jacob Kane.

"You don't know how badly I need this..."

Lenses in mask similar to Batwoman's

Gauntlets equipped with flamethrowers

Costume possibly inspired by Nightwing's

Protective suit fitted with functioning wings

CATWOMAN

VITAL STATS

Real Name: Selina Kyle

Occupation: Crime boss and thief, sometime hero, owner of Egyptian Casino

Height: 1.70 m

Weight: 58 kg

Base: Gotham City

Allies: Killer Croc, the Justice League of America, Batman, Inc., Alice Tesla

Foes: The Joker's Daughter, Bone, Black Mask

POWERS AND ABILITIES

Master cat burglar; expert fighter; accomplished gymnast. Weapons include cat-o-nine-tails whip and gloves with diamond-tipped claws.

GIVING BACK

Selina Kyle learnt to steal at an early age while living at an orphanage. She became an expert cat burglar, but retains a strict moral code that compels her to protect the underprivileged, often joining forces with Batman.

Selina Kyle's father is the notorious former Gotham City crime boss, Rex "the Lion" Calabrese. She unknowingly began to follow in his footsteps after being thrown from a rooftop when investigating her own past. She crafted a Catwoman costume out of the awning that saved her life, later rising up the ranks of the underworld to become a crime boss herself.

"In case you hadn't noticed, I don't fight crime, I am crime."

Many gadgets devised by Alice Tesla

Belt doubles as a whip

Bodysuit allows freedom of movement

THE BIRDS OF PREY

VITAL STATS

Team Name: The Birds of Prey
Base: Gotham City
Allies: Batman, the Batman Family, Mother Eve
Foes: The Penguin, Mr Freeze, Rā's al Ghūl

Members: Batgirl, Black Canary, Katana, Strix, Condor, Poison Ivy (traitor), Starling (traitor)

ENEMIES AND FRENEMIES

The Birds of Prey fought several villains including Mr Freeze, Rā's al Ghūl, and even former teammate, Poison Ivy. Team members often had trouble seeing eye to eye, eventually leading to the team's disbandment.

After serving time as an agent with the Team 7 government strike force, Canary (Dinah Lance) went solo. She changed her name to Black Canary and gained employment at the Iceberg Casino to break up a deal between the Penguin and terrorist organisation Basilisk. During this operation she met Starling and Batgirl, who would later join forces with her as the Birds of Prey.

"...Nobody on this team has a squeaky-clean soul."

Strix was brought onto the team by Batgirl

Black Canary relished serving on a new team

Batgirl took over as leader after Black Canary

Batgirl eventually disbanded the Birds

BLACK CANARY

VITAL STATS

Real Name: Dinah Drake Lance

Occupation: Hero, singer

Height: 1.63 m

Weight: 52 kg

Base: Mobile

Allies: Batgirl, the Birds of Prey, Batman

Foes: Basilisk, Rā's al Ghūl, the Penguin

POWERS AND ABILITIES

Expert martial artist with advanced military training; intelligent and an excellent strategist; natural leader; Canary Cry strong enough to shatter walls; well connected in the intelligence and Super Hero worlds.

A LIFE LESS ORDINARY

Black Canary lives a life of endless changes. After a long stint with the crime fighters called the Birds of Prey, she decided to go solo, and found herself the lead singer of her own band, aptly named Black Canary.

Uses powerful voice to headline band

Abandoned as a child, Dinah Drake found a home at a dojo (martial arts school) in Gotham City, where she trained until she was discovered by the US government. She joined special ops group Team 7, where she took part in genetic testing and discovered her Canary Cry — the ability to deliver an ultrasonic scream. Dinah later went freelance as Super Hero Black Canary.

"We've got a big day tomorrow. Rock 'n' roll."

Recently started wearing punk rock attire

Extremely athletic and agile

LADY BLACKHAWK

VITAL STATS

Real Name: Zinda Blake°

Occupation: Hero, pilot

Height: 1.70 m

Weight: 53 kg

Base: Mobile

Allies: The Birds of Prey, Blackhawks

Foes: The Penguin, Killer Shark

POWERS AND ABILITIES

Expert pilot, who can handle any kind of aircraft with ease; adept hand-to-hand combatant; proficient marksman.

BLACKHAWK DOWN

Zinda Blake has never been one to back down from a challenge, and more often than not can be found brawling in whatever bar she's chosen to drink in on any particular night. Nevertheless, she became a valued ally to the Birds of Prey.

Sign up at recruitment center near you.

Lady Blackhawk was a member of the Blackhawks, a secretive squadron of ace pilots who fought during World War II. After travelling through time, Lady Blackhawk temporarily served as a pilot for the Birds of Prey. More unruly than her fellow Super Heroes, Lady Blackhawk has nevertheless proven that she can hold her own in nearly any fight.

Pilot jacket is flexible to allow ease of movement

Old fashioned costume shows difficulty adjusting to modern times

Wears traditional Blackhawk symbol

"Gonna be one beautiful flight."

STRIX

VITAL STATS

Real Name: Mary Turner

Occupation: Hero, former assassin

Height: 1.70 m

Weight: 54 kg

Base: Gotham City

Allies: Batgirl, the Birds of Prey, Talon, the Secret Six

Foes: The Court of Owls, Mr Freeze, Rās al Ghūl

POWERS AND ABILITIES

Expert assassin and fighter trained by the Court of Owls; natural acrobat; genius IQ; extremely observant; possesses healing factor and can "die" and be brought back to life again.

ROUGH START

After encountering Batgirl during a battle against the Court of Owls, Strix was recruited to join the Birds of Prey. There was some friction between the teammates at first, but she soon became a trusted member of their entourage.

During an attack on the United States by Japan in 1944, a girl named Mary was badly scarred, losing her tongue as well as her family. She found work at Haly's Circus, but despite being a talented aerialist, she stayed behind the scenes as her face frightened audiences. She was recruited by the Court of Owls, but broke free of their influence thanks to Batgirl.

"Hrrrnnn!"

Altered costume slightly to fool the Court of Owls

Does not speak, just grunts

Clawed fingertips on gloves

CONDOR

VITAL STATS

Real Name:
Benjamin Reyes

Occupation: Hero,
former terrorist agent

Height: 1.83 m

Weight: 90 kg

Base: Gotham City

Allies: The Birds of Prey,
Mother Eve

Foes: Strike Force Basilisk,
Regulus

POWERS AND ABILITIES

Telekinetic abilities can
produce energy blasts
or shields; flight; armoured
battle suit; expert at
various languages.

FLIGHT OF THE CONDOR

Condor turned his criminal life around to
become the sole male member of the Birds
of Prey. He encountered the Birds while
in Japan, and grew quite fond of Black
Canary, hoping for a romance with her.

Mind can
produce energy
blasts or shields

Flight powered
by telekinetic
abilities

Ben Reyes lost his security job due to
crippling headaches. He couldn't bear
the pain, but he was soon taken in
by Tsiklon, a member of the terrorist
organisation Basilisk. Ben realised
his pains were just his growing
powers. He learnt later how
corrupt his Basilisk saviours were
and quit their team, changing his
codename from Poltergeist to Condor.

Armoured battle suit
built by a Basilisk
prisoner that
Condor rescued

"I'm good at catching bullets."

BATMAN, INC.

VITAL STATS

Team Name: Batman, Inc.

Base: Gotham City and various countries around the globe

Allies: Batman, the Batman Family, Batwoman, Wayne Enterprises

Foes: Talia al Ghūl, Scorpiana, Heretic

Members: Batman, Robin, Red Robin, Catwoman, Dick Grayson, Batgirl, Batwing, Batwing (Luke Fox), Nightrunner, Batman Japan, Wingman, the Knight (Cyril Sheldrake) (deceased), the Knight (formerly the Squire), El Gaucho, Man-of-Bats, Hood, Raven Red, Dark Ranger, Black Bat, Metamorpho, Katana, Halo, Looker, Freight Train, the Huntress, Batman of Moscow (deceased)

INCORPORATING THE WORLD

Batman, Incorporated succeeded in establishing officially licenced Batmen around the world, protecting countries as diverse as France, Japan and Russia. The team even found an unofficial mascot in the form of Bat-Cow.

After a brush with death, Batman learnt of a new threat to the world in the secret society called Leviathan. Using funding from Wayne Enterprises, Bruce Wayne publicly launched Batman, Incorporated, a mission to place a "Batman" in various cities around the globe. While it cost him the lives of a few members, Batman, Inc. was a success that ended Leviathan's threat.

Batman led Batman, Inc., even after it was banned from activity in Gotham City

The Squire graduated to become the Knight after the death of her partner

"Ladies and gentlemen. I give you Batman, Incorporated!"

EL GAUCHO

VITAL STATS

Real Name: Santiago Vargas

Occupation: Hero, wealthy socialite

Height: 1.85 m

Weight: 97.5 kg

Base: Buenos Aires, Argentina

Allies: Batman, Batman, Inc., the Club of Heroes

Foes: The Club of Villains, Leviathan, Dr Hurt, Scorpiana, El Sombrero

POWERS AND ABILITIES

Highly trained hand-to-hand combatant; usually drives motorcycle during missions; intelligent and extremely wealthy.

THE MARK OF GAUCHO

El Gaucho and Batman once teamed up to track down Dr Dedalus, a Spyral agent. The Dark Knight's respect for El Gaucho is perhaps due to him seeing a bit of his childhood hero, Zorro, in the crime fighter.

In the early days of Batman's career, billionaire John Mayhew recruited him to be part of the Club of Heroes alongside other international crime fighters. While Batman didn't find the Club to his liking, he later enlisted many of its members into his own team, Batman, Inc., including El Gaucho, who represented his native country, Argentina.

"...the tango of death is over!"

El Gaucho was secretly Agent 33 for Spyral. However, he turned on his boss, Dr Dedalus, and saved Batman's life.

THE KNIGHT

VITAL STATS

Real Name: Cyril Sheldrake

Occupation: Hero

Height: 1.88 m

Weight: 95 kg

Base: Wordenshire, England

Allies: The Squire, the Knight I, Batman, Batman, Inc., the Club of Heroes

Foes: Springheeled Jack, Morris Men, Leviathan, Heretic

POWERS AND ABILITIES

Expert martial artist; skilled detective and gymnast; impressive intellect; armoured suit equipped with myriad devices; natural born leader; vast supply of vehicles and weapons.

KNIGHT IN WAITING
The Knight and his partner, the Squire, were fairly inseparable, often spending time at their favourite pub, the Time in a Bottle. When the Knight was killed, the Squire took his place after mourning her old friend.

Cyril Sheldrake used to be known as the Squire — a loyal sidekick to his father Percy, the original Knight. The pair were the so-called Batman and Robin of England. As the Squire, he joined the Club of Heroes with his father. Later graduating to the position of the Knight, Cyril would become a member of Batman, Inc., and perish in a deadly battle with the Heretic.

"Don't let them win, Beryl..."

Being the Knight was a family tradition, which Cyril took on gladly. He stepped into his father's large shoes, and made the role of the Knight his own.

THE SQUIRE

VITAL STATS

Real Name: Beryl Hutchinson
Occupation: Hero
Height: 1.65 m
Weight: 50 kg
Base: Wordenshire, England
Allies: The Knight II, Batman, Inc., Dark Ranger II, Red Robin
Foes: Springheeled Jack, Morris Men, Leviathan, Heretic

POWERS AND ABILITIES

Expert martial artist; skilled detective and gymnast; impressive intellect; armoured suit equipped with myriad offensive and defensive devices; natural born leader; vast supply of vehicles and weapons.

TRAVELLING SQUIRE

Though based in England, the Squire had been to Gotham City several times, as the Squire, then as the Knight. An adept crime fighter, she is even more determined now that her mentor has died.

After discovering the secret identity of the Knight, Beryl Hutchinson helped the hero against his foe, Springheeled Jack, and was sworn in as the Knight's Squire. As a member of Batman, Inc., the Squire helped recruit her ally and future love interest, Dark Ranger, before taking the mantle of the Knight following her partner's death.

"I wasn't taking this seriously enough but I am now."

After her mentor was killed, the Squire stepped up to be the third hero to be known as the Knight, lashing out at the forces of Leviathan.

MAN-OF-BATS

VITAL STATS

Real Name: Dr William Great Eagle
Occupation: Hero, doctor
Height: 1.85 m
Weight: 101.5 kg
Base: South Dakota
Allies: Raven Red, Batman, Inc., the Club of Heroes
Foes: The Club of Villains, Leviathan, Dr Hurt

POWERS AND ABILITIES

Highly trained hand-to-hand combatant; intelligent and trained as a medical doctor; expert archer and horseback rider; efficient with many traditional Native American weapons; runs imitation Batcave/tourist attraction.

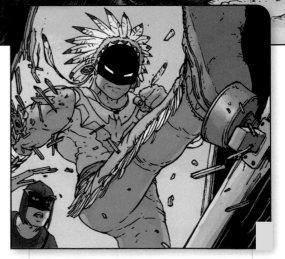

RIDING INTO THE SUNSET
Both Man-of-Bats and his sidekick and son, Raven Red, have teamed with Batman. Batman visited their small town when Leviathan targeted Man-of-Bats due to his association with the Dark Knight.

One of the many Batman-inspired crime fighters to join the Club of Heroes, Man-of-Bats fights for justice on a Native American reservation in South Dakota. While he has modelled himself after the Dark Knight, Man-of-Bats prefers to employ traditional Native American weapons and dress, displaying them alongside his trophies in his own "Bat's Cave".

Man-of-Bats's actions have been an issue for law enforcement as he acts fast in emergencies, but doesn't always consider the consequences.

"Better send a Bat-Signal."

RAVEN RED

VITAL STATS

Real Name: Charles Great Eagle

Occupation: Hero

Height: 1.75 m

Weight: 76 kg

Base: South Dakota

Allies: Man-of-Bats, Batman, Inc., the Club of Heroes

Foes: The Club of Villains, Leviathan, Dr Hurt

POWERS AND ABILITIES

Highly trained hand-to-hand combatant; highly intelligent; expert archer, horseback rider and efficient with traditional Native American weapons; helps run imitation Batcave tourist attraction; wears bullet-repelling "ghost shirt".

LITTLE BIG MAN

Raven Red used to be called Little Raven, a name he grew out of during his crime-fighting career. He has yet to truly emerge from his father's shadow, however, and remains Man-of-Bats's steadfast partner.

The son of Man-of-Bats, Raven Red was disappointed in his father for leaving San Francisco after Raven's mother died. He soon began to recognise the nobility in his father's mission to protect their ancestral home. Even so, he has felt that he was personally destined for something bigger, like a membership in the Teen Titans.

"We can handle this our way, like we always do."

Raven Red wears the "Ghost Shirt". His father once sat outside a museum for days in order to reclaim the shirt for his Bat's Cave museum.

BATMAN JAPAN

VITAL STATS

Real Name: Jiro Osamu

Occupation: Hero

Height: 1.78 m

Weight: 78.5 kg

Base: Tokyo, Japan

Allies: Mr Unknown, Batman, Inc., Lolita Canary

Foes: Lord Death Man, Leviathan, Doubleface, Lady Tiger Fist, Dr Inside-Out

POWERS AND ABILITIES

Highly skilled martial artist and acrobat; trained by the original Mr Unknown; wears protective costume equipped with hi-tech gadgets; employs cutting edge weapons and vehicles supplied by Batman, Inc.

LIFE AFTER DEATH

To become Batman Japan, Jiro faked his death as the hero Mr Unknown. It was his way of starting fresh and beginning his own legacy. He later set up his own base, a hideout modelled after that of his hero and ally, Batman.

Jiro Osamu was the assistant to the Japanese hero Mr Unknown, his "body double" of sorts. While Mr Unknown was the brains of the operation, Jiro did the physical part: patrols, stakeouts and street fighting. When Mr Unknown was killed by Lord Death Man, Jiro stepped up as the new Mr Unknown. He was soon asked to join Batman, Inc. as Batman Japan.

"Guns are for cowards."

Batman Japan's costumes have changed frequently over the years, He employs his current look when teaming up with his girlfriend, Lolita Canary.

NIGHTRUNNER

VITAL STATS

Real Name: Bilal Asselah
Occupation: Hero
Height: 1.78 m
Weight: 75.5 kg
Base: Paris, France
Allies: Batman, Inc.,
Batman, Dick Grayson
Foes: Leviathan, La Muerte
en Vida, the Man Who Laughs

POWERS AND ABILITIES

Expert at parkour free-
running; highly acrobatic;
trained in hand-to-hand
combat by Dick Grayson;
extremely athletic and
fast; access to Batman,
Inc. equipment and funds;
Utility Belt includes a
grapnel gun.

RUNNING MAN

When Batman and Dick Grayson helped
curb riots in Paris caused by bizarre
assassinations, Nightrunner caught their
eye. He was soon deputised as a Batman,
Inc. member, and later replaced the retired
Musketeer as the Batman of France.

A Sunni Muslim born in the outskirts
of Paris, France, Bilal Asselah lost a
friend during a riot in his neighbourhood,
experiencing firsthand the horror of
violence. Out of frustration, he started
running over the rooftops. Soon,
people began to notice his dynamic
runs. With the makings of a local hero,
he adopted the name Nightrunner and
sought to curb the violence of his city.

*"Well, I guess If we've
already got the suit..."*

Adopted mask
when he started
getting noticed

Altered shirt
as a nod to
Batman

Toned physique
from countless
rooftop runs

Utility Belt
stocked with
helpful gadgets

BLACK BAT

VITAL STATS

Real Name: Cassandra Cain
Occupation: Hero
Height: 1.65 m
Weight: 50 kg
Base: Gotham City
Allies: Batman, Batman, Inc., Red Robin
Foes: David Cain, Leviathan, Lady Shiva

POWERS AND ABILITIES

One of the best martial artists in the world; able to read the body language of others and predict their next move; incredibly athletic with quick reflexes; trained by an expert assassin; Utility Belt full of useful devices; access to Batman, Inc. equipment.

SILENT PREDATOR

Black Bat is a natural fighter whose abilities were magnified when her father, David Cain, refused to teach her how to talk. Instead, she learnt to communicate through body language and violence.

The daughter of assassin David Cain and Lady Shiva, Cassandra Cain was born with a natural aptitude towards athletics and the fighting arts. Raised by her father, Cassandra perfected his assassin skills at an early age, and once even killed for him. Realising this was wrong, Cassandra fled from her father and wound up in Gotham City, later adopting the identity of Black Bat.

"I think I've always liked it in Gotham."

Joining Batman's allies proved beneficial for Cassandra. She learnt to speak, and also became a valued member of Batman, Inc.

THE HOOD

VITAL STATS

Real Name: George Cross
Occupation: Hero, spy
Height: 1.78 m
Weight: 78 kg
Base: London, England
Allies: Batman, Batman, Inc., Spyral, T.H.E.Y.
Foes: Leviathan, Dr Dedalus

POWERS AND ABILITIES

Highly trained hand-to-hand combatant and martial artist; athletic and agile; expert spy; access to Batman, Inc. equipment as well as his own Hood-themed car; fully stocked Utility Belt; excellent detective skills.

PICK A SIDE

The Hood kept his involvement in the clandestine organisation known as Spyral a secret from his Batman, Inc. cohorts. However, the Hood was fighting on Batman's side all along, especially when it came to his opposition of Leviathan.

Styles himself after Robin Hood

Costume based on medieval knight armour

Cross logo hints at his real name

Inspired by Robin Hood, George Cross takes money from criminals and gives it to the poor. When Batman first met the Hood in London, he was impressed, and he thought of the British hero when he later formed Batman, Inc. The Hood accepted the Dark Knight's offer to join the organisation, and used the opportunity to become a triple agent, working for England's Super Secret Service (T.H.E.Y.) and Spyral.

"World's greatest assassins... meet Batman's front line."

DARK RANGER

VITAL STATS

Real Name: Johnny Riley

Occupation: Hero

Height: 1.78 m

Weight: 82 kg

Base: Melbourne, Australia

Allies: Batman, Inc., Dark Ranger I, Batman, the Squire

Foes: Leviathan, La Muerte en Vida

POWERS AND ABILITIES

Utilises armoured suit inherited from the original Dark Ranger; jet pack enables flight; carries pistol that fires electro-stun blasts; uniform has pouches that contain various hi-tech gadgets and weapons.

PEP TALK

Dark Ranger was sworn into Batman, Inc. by Batman himself. Always a bit cynical, Riley was convinced to give Batman, Inc. a try by the Squire, and the two even became romantically involved.

Johnny Riley used to be the Super Hero sidekick to the Ranger — the Australian version of Batman. As the years passed, the Ranger became the Dark Ranger and Scout gave up the heroic life. However, when the Dark Ranger was murdered, Riley donned his mentor's suit and took up the mantle of the Dark Ranger. He was soon recruited into Batman, Inc.

"You gotta let me try out one of your batarangs."

The original Ranger traded in a boy scout look for riot gear. The second Dark Ranger, Johnny Riley, follows suit, carrying an array of non-lethal weapons.

BAT-MITE

NEUTRAL

VITAL STATS

Real Name: Unknown
Occupation: Other-dimensional imp, self-proclaimed hero
Height: 0.89 m
Weight: 21.5 kg
Base: Gotham City
Allies: Batman, the Batman Family, Booster Gold
Foes: Gridlock, Dr Trauma

POWERS AND ABILITIES

Flight; teleportation; can change clothing or appearance of others; wears Utility Belt filled with gadgets, including a bat-shaped cellphone, shield and a laser.

THE DARK-MITE RETURNS

After escaping death by drowning at the hands of Dr Trauma's lackeys, Bat-Mite returned to the villain's hideout. He prevented Trauma from switching her mind with that of the hero Hawkman.

More of a nuisance than a threat or an ally, Bat-Mite has labelled himself Batman's number one fan. In fact, in his warped mind, he is the hero and Batman is merely his sidekick. Bat-Mite comes from another dimension and he has some magical powers, but he treats crime fighting like a game, and often prevents Batman from stopping villains in an efficient fashion.

"All in a day's work for a champion of justice."

Batman was not happy when the imp hijacked the Batmobile and sped it over a ravine. Yet he still stopped the criminals Bat-Mite was pursuing.

TITUS

VITAL STATS

Full Name: Titus

Occupation:
Robin's pet

Height: 0.94 m

Weight: 63.5 kg

Base: Gotham City

Allies: Robin, the Batman
Family, Alfred Pennyworth

Foes: Apokolips soldiers,
Kalibak

POWERS AND ABILITIES

Purebred Great Dane;
excellent sense of smell
and hearing; fiercely loyal
to the Batman Family;
brave and known to
rush head first into
battle; fit and trim.

HOUND OF THE APOKOLIPS

Titus tagged along to Apokolips when
Batman, Red Robin, Nightwing, Batgirl
and Red Hood invaded the planet to
retrieve the temporarily dead body of
Robin. Titus held his own, taking out
vicious attack dogs.

Bruce Wayne noticed that his son
Damian was having a hard time
transitioning into the life of a Super
Hero, so he bought a Great Dane to
serve as the boy's pet. When Damian
eventually took to the animal, he
named it Titus and the dog has been
his loyal friend ever since. Damian
then adopted more animals, including
a cat named Alfred.

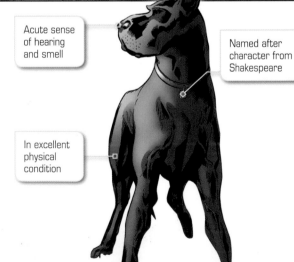

Acute sense
of hearing
and smell

Named after
character from
Shakespeare

In excellent
physical
condition

"Rrarf."

BAT-COW

VITAL STATS

Full Name: Bat-Cow

Occupation: Robin's pet

Height: 1.52 m

Weight: 568 kg

Base: Gotham City

Allies: Robin, Alfred Pennyworth, the Batman Family

Foes: Meat eaters

POWERS AND ABILITIES
Average female Guernsey cow.

BAT-ZOO
While the pets in the Batcave are supposed to belong to Robin, Alfred Pennyworth seems to take on the lion's share of the work when it comes to feeding and caring for Bat-Cow, whether he's happy about it or not.

Robin and Batman were fighting villains in a slaughterhouse, when they realised it was an ambush. An assassin called Goatboy had tried and failed to destroy Robin. Taking pity on the last remaining cow, Robin declared himself a vegetarian and took the animal home with him. With mask-like colouring on his face and a star brand on his rump, Bat-Cow became Robin's newest pet.

"Moo!"

After Robin was killed by the villain Heretic, then brought back to life, he returned to the Batcave, happy that Alfred had taken care of his pets.

THOMAS WAYNE

VITAL STATS

Full Name: Thomas Wayne

Occupation: Surgeon, philanthropist

Height: 1.88 m

Weight: 95 kg

Base: Gotham City

Allies: Martha and Bruce Wayne, Alfred and Jarvis Pennyworth, Lucius Fox

Foes: Joe Chill, the Court of Owls

POWERS AND ABILITIES

Highly skilled surgeon; powerful connections in the business world; amateur mechanic and inventor; extremely intelligent and loving father.

THE LAST NIGHT
Thomas and Martha Wayne's fate was sealed the night they took their son to a screening of The Mark of Zorro in Gotham City. After the film, they were shot dead by Joe Chill during a botched robbery.

Thomas Wayne was a loving husband and father. Born into a wealthy family, Thomas created quite a career for himself as a surgeon. Though he was killed when his son Bruce was just a boy, he had nevertheless created many memories with his son, including showing Bruce a Witch's Eye, a hi-tech visual mapping device that later helped inspire the creation of the Batman.

> *"What do you love about Gotham, Bruce?"*

Hat bears logo similar to Robin's

Wears casual attire in spare time when tinkering with mechanics

Doted on his son, often giving gifts

MARTHA WAYNE

VITAL STATS

Full Name: Martha Wayne
Occupation: Mother, philanthropist
Height: 1.63 m
Weight: 49 kg
Base: Gotham City
Allies: Thomas and Bruce Wayne, Alfred and Jarvis Pennyworth
Foes: Joe Chill, the Court of Owls

POWERS AND ABILITIES

Empathetic philanthropist; powerful contacts in Gotham City's most elite social circles, partially due to Kane family name (Martha's maiden name); intelligent and giving mother.

MOTHER OF INNOVATION

Martha Wayne, a civic-minded woman, was upset at the state of Gotham City's education system. To fix the problem, she created a new school for Gotham City's underprivileged, despite receiving threats from the mayor's office.

A loving mother to Bruce Wayne, Martha Wayne was a philanthropist who stood up to Gotham City's corrupt mayor's office, not knowing it was backed by the violent, secret organisation, the Court of Owls. The Court of Owls caused Martha to have a car "accident". and her loyal butler Jarvis Pennyworth was killed by a Talon assassin as well.

"You're the bravest boy in Gotham, Bruce."

While her life was full of tragedy, and would soon end thanks to Joe Chill, Martha spent much of her short life doting on her son, Bruce.

JAMES GORDON

VITAL STATS

Full Name: James W. Gordon

Occupation: Deputised vigilante, former police commissioner

Height: 1.75 m

Weight: 76 kg

Base: Gotham City

Allies: Batman, the Batman Family, Batgirl, G.C.P.D.

Foes: The Joker, Mr Bloom, James Gordon, Jr

POWERS AND ABILITIES

Extremely physically fit; natural leader; expertise in police procedure; former marine; robotic suit armed with crime-fighting equipment.

BATMAN 2.0

After the real Batman seemingly died, James Gordon stepped up to fill the role as a fully deputised agent of the law. Wearing a Batsuit inside a giant bat-themed robot suit, the 46-year-old does his best to fill Batman's shoes.

Haircut harks back to his days as a Marine

Shaved moustache to resemble Batman

Highly trained fighter

Got back in shape to become Batman

James Gordon worked his way up the chain of command at the Gotham City Police Department, fighting corruption at every turn. He eventually became commissioner, but was framed for murder and incarcerated. Gordon's job was not waiting for him when he was exonerated. However, he accepted an offer from Geri Powers to become the G.C.P.D.'s official Batman instead.

"Sometimes, you just have to get out and walk the beat."

MAGGIE SAWYER

VITAL STATS

Full Name: Margaret Sawyer

Occupation: Commissioner of the G.C.P.D.

Height: 1.70 m

Weight: 59 kg

Base: Gotham City

Allies: Batwoman, G.C.P.D., Superman

Foes: Nocturna, Ceto

POWERS AND ABILITIES

Excellent detective and commanding officer; expert knowledge of police procedure and policy; natural leader with strong moral compass; trained in hand-to-hand combat as well as with a firearm.

ONE GOOD COP

Maggie Sawyer is a tough cop who has worked her way up the career ladder through honest police work. She promoted fellow honest cop, Harvey Bullock, to leader of the newly established Batman task force.

Commissioner Maggie Sawyer got her start in police work as an officer in the Metropolis Police Department. She got her first real taste of Gotham City when she was bused to the city with fellow officers to assist during a superstorm and citywide blackout. It was there she met her future fiancée Kate Kane for the first time — who would also go on to become Batwoman.

"I'll do my best for your city."

Wears bulletproof vest when needed

Dresses casually, but business appropriate

Excellent marksman, not afraid to shoot

HARVEY BULLOCK

VITAL STATS

Full Name: Harvey Bullock
Occupation: G.C.P.D. detective
Height: 1.78 m
Weight: 112 kg
Base: Gotham City
Allies: James Gordon, G.C.P.D., Renee Montoya, Batman
Foes: Anarky, the Joker's Daughter, Dr Death

POWERS AND ABILITIES

Excellent detective; good fighter with street smarts; loyal friend to James Gordon; one of the few honest cops in Gotham City.

BULLOCK'S LAW

As a rookie police officer, Bullock worked with James Gordon on several cases, including the emergence of Dr Death. As a detective, he's come into his own, and is respected throughout the G.C.P.D.

Harvey Bullock, who has been working for the G.C.P.D. since the infamous citywide blackout, is one of Gotham City's clean cops, even if his appearance doesn't quite match his resumé. While he and Batman don't always see eye to eye, Bullock often worked with the Dark Knight, and now teams with the Dark Knight's successor, James Gordon, as head of Batman's task force team.

"I don't trust anyone... except you, Jimbo."

Harvey trained G.C.P.D. officer Renee Montoya and they became friends – before she moved to Blüdhaven. She has since returned.

RENEE MONTOYA

VITAL STATS

Full Name: Renee Montoya
Occupation: G.C.P.D. detective
Height: 1.73 m
Weight: 65.5 kg
Base: Gotham City
Allies: Harvey Bullock, Batman, James Gordon, Batwoman
Foes: Detective Nancy Yip, the Joker's Daughter

POWERS AND ABILITIES

Highly trained police detective; trained by Harvey Bullock; experienced fighter with good hand-to-hand combat skills.

A QUESTION OF ETHICS

While Renee Montoya has proven herself an honest police officer and fiercely loyal to other good cops, she's not above the occasional bar brawl. Especially when those she's trading punches with are known criminals.

In the **Gotham City** Police Department, it can often be hard to find cops on the right side of the law. While things have improved over the years thanks to James Gordon, that wasn't always the case. Corruption was rife in the department when Renee Montoya first started out, but she was determined to make a difference, aided and abetted by her instructor, Harvey Bullock.

"...you know how sacred partnerships are."

Back in Gotham City after years in Blüdhaven, Montoya wanted to root out corruption, and found an enemy in Detective Nancy Yip.

G.C.P.D.

ALLIES

VITAL STATS

Official Name: Gotham City
Police Department
Base: Gotham City
Allies: Batman, the Batman
Family, Batwoman
Foes: Criminals, Arkham
Asylum inmates, Blackgate
Penitentiary prisoners

Notable Members: James
Gordon, Maggie Sawyer,
Harvey Bullock, Renee
Montoya, Carlos Alvarez,
Travis Nie, Tammy Keyes,
Jim Corrigan, Melody
McKenna, Henry Wallace,
Nancy Strode, Jack Forbes
(former), Jason Bard
(former), Nancy Yip (former),
Gillian B. Loeb (former)

POWER PLAY
Perhaps the best known
commissioner in Gotham City's
history, James Gordon was
recently framed for a crime he
didn't commit, and jailed until
his eventual pardon. He now
serves in the Batman task force
under Commissioner Sawyer.

The Gotham City Police Department
has a reputation for being corrupt.
However, James Gordon has
significantly curbed the institution's
own criminal population. Now operating
under the incorruptible commissioner,
Maggie Sawyer, the G.C.P.D. employs
dedicated men and women who are
constantly at odds with the city's most
notorious criminals, like Catwoman.

*"...Gotham isn't like any other
city... We need Batman."*

Left to right: Detective Harvey Bullock,
Commissioner Maggie Sawyer and former
commissioners Jack Forbes and Jason Bard.

46

THE MIDNIGHT SHIFT

VITAL STATS

Real Name: Precinct 13

Base: Gotham City

Allies: Batman, G.C.P.D.

Foe: Gentleman Ghost

Members: Lieutenant Sam Weaver, Detective Jim Corrigan, Detective Lisa Drake, Dr Szandor Tarr, Sister Justine (deceased)

THE 13TH PRECINCT

The G.C.P.D.'s most mysterious division, Precinct 13 is also referred to as the Midnight Shift. When its methods came into question, Sergeant Rook from internal affairs was assigned to assess the team.

The Midnight Shift was formed by Gotham City's former police commissioner, Jim Gordon. With its own discretionary budget, the task force was assembled to take care of "detailed cases". They deal with supernatural situations too bizarre for normal police officers, from battling mysterious entities, such as the Gentleman Ghost, to freeing possessed school children.

> *"We're the guys who handle the strange stuff."*

Batman is aware of Jim Corrigan's dark secret: that he is host to Spectre, the angel of vengeance, and fights a daily battle to contain the spirit.

LUCIUS FOX

VITAL STATS

Full Name: Lucius Fox
Occupation: CEO of
Wayne Enterprises
Height: 1.83 m
Weight: 90 kg
Base: Gotham City
Allies: Batman and Bruce
Wayne, Batwing, the
Batman Family
Foes: Clayface, Ratcatcher,
Menace

POWERS AND ABILITIES

Savvy inventor and
electronics expert;
extremely intelligent and
loyal to the Wayne family;
near unlimited access to
Wayne Enterprises' assets;
financial genius.

BATMAN BEYOND
When Fox was kidnapped
by Clayface, Bruce Wayne
saved his life with the help
of an incredible prototype
Batsuit. Unfortunately, Fox
claimed that it wouldn't be
cost effective for 20 years.

While Lucius Fox spends most of his
time running the day to day operations
of Bruce Wayne's huge company, he
maintains a healthy interest in the
Research & Development department,
working with Batman to help the Dark
Knight stay technologically innovative.
Lucius is also the father of the hero
Batwing, although he is unaware of
his son Luke's crime-fighting career.

Inventor's mind has
designed much of
Batman's equipment

Unassuming
appearance
masks
incredible
intellect

Business attire for
many important
meetings

*"You came back to a city about
five minutes before it collapsed."*

GERI POWERS

VITAL STATS

Full Name: Geri Powers

Occupation: CEO of Powers International

Height: 1.65 m

Weight: 54 kg

Base: Gotham City

Allies: .G.C.P.D, James Gordon

Foe: Mayor Sebastian Hady

POWERS AND ABILITIES

CEO of one of the most powerful businesses in Gotham City and the world; oversees the technology for G.C.P.D.'s Batman project; powerful police and business connections; highly intelligent and motivated.

THE POWER BEHIND THE BATMAN

Geri Powers oversaw the creation and implementation of the robotic armoured Batsuit that James Gordon pilots in conjunction with the Gotham City Police Department. She helps Gordon get used to his new role and is his biggest supporter.

Gordon agreed to adopt the mantle of Batman after Powers pointed out that none of the G.C.P.D.'s recruits would be the "right" Batman.

Powers International has been one of the most important corporations in Gotham City for centuries. After Wayne Enterprises was made defunct during a scheme launched by Lincoln March and the Cluemaster, Powers acquired the company and its assets. CEO Geri Powers gave the G.C.P.D. the technology to create a Batman of its own when the real Batman was presumed dead.

> "Are you ready to be Batman... Commissioner Gordon?"

PHILIP KANE

NEUTRAL

VITAL STATS

Full Name: Philip Kane

Occupation: Former Wayne Enterprises CEO

Height: 1.80 m

Weight: 83.5 kg

Base: Gotham City

Allies: The Riddler, Bruce Wayne, Martha Wayne

Foes: The Red Hood Gang

POWERS AND ABILITIES

Access to Wayne Enterprises funds and technology; criminal ties to the Red Hood Gang; held powerful business connections; gifted eye for business; advised by Edward Nygma.

KANE AND ABLE

The brother of Bruce Wayne's mother, Martha Wayne, Philip Kane had been trying to track Bruce down for years. Kane eventually located Bruce at his base, a townhouse near Crime Alley, the street where the Waynes were killed.

When Thomas and Martha Wayne were murdered and their son Bruce left to travel the world, Philip Kane was put in charge of the family business and merged Kane Chemical and Wayne Industries. On Bruce's return to Gotham City, he found out his uncle was working with the Red Hood Gang. After Kane's death at the hands of Red Hood One, Bruce reclaimed his company.

On the night Batman foiled the Red Hood Gang's raid of A.C.E. Chemical, Philip Kane was killed by Red Hood One after trying to save Batman.

> *"I never meant for things to turn out this way."*

HENRI DUCARD

VITAL STATS

Full Name: Henri Ducard
Occupation: Mercenary
Height: 1.73 m
Weight: 74.5 kg
Base: Paris, France
Allies: NoBody
Foe: Batman

POWERS AND ABILITIES

One of the world's best manhunters; expert in many lethal weapons as well as in hand-to-hand combat; numerous connections in the intelligence and criminal world.

ETHICAL DISPUTES

Bruce Wayne discovered that he didn't always agree with his mentor's methods. During Bruce's training, they tracked down a terrorist named Hassan. Ducard assassinated Hassan instead of handing him over to the authorities, a decision Bruce did not approve of.

Henri Ducard was an accomplished manhunter, perhaps the best in the world. So unsurprisingly, when Bruce Wayne was training to become Batman, he sought out Ducard as one of his instructors. Henri agreed to train Wayne, seeing something he liked in the young man. He taught Bruce how to track and locate a man, a skill Batman has used throughout his career.

"...it costs a lot to play in my game..."

After the assassination of Hassan, Bruce ended his training with Ducard. Ducard was furious and sent his son, Morgan, to kill him.

DUKE THOMAS

HERO

VITAL STATS

Full Name: Duke Thomas

Occupation: Hero

Height: 1.86 m

Weight: 58.5 kg

Base: Gotham City

Allies: Batman, Alfred Pennyworth, fellow Robins, Julie Madison, Leslie Thompkins

Foes: The Joker, the Riddler

POWERS AND ABILITIES

Incredibly intelligent and a good problem solver; natural leader; athletic and a good hand-to-hand combatant; access to Robin equipment and the Nest network.

A DEBT OF GRATITUDE

After regaining consciousness after being cared for by Duke's family, Batman saved Duke Thomas from masked criminals. It was his way of paying the boy back for the kindness his family had shown him.

Duke Thomas first met Bruce Wayne during Gotham City's infamous blackout. With the Riddler taking control of the city, Duke's family nursed Wayne back to health and young Duke tried to devise a way to defeat the villain. Years later, Duke and Batman's met again when the Joker went after Duke's parents. Duke later went on to become Robin.

"Don't you guys have professionals to do this kind of stuff?!"

Each Robin wears colours in a unique way

Still thinks about, and searches for, his missing parents

Joined up with team of Robins led by Alfred

VICKI VALE

ALLY

VITAL STATS

Full Name: Vicki Vale

Occupation: Journalist for the *Gotham Gazette*

Height: 1.73 m

Weight: 52 kg

Base: Gotham City

Allies: Bruce Wayne, Jason Bard, Warren Stacey

Foes: The Penguin, Carmine Falcone

POWERS AND ABILITIES

Ace reporter with a knack for finding major news stories; extremely intelligent and a detective in her own right; athletic and capable of self-defence against attackers.

HANDS ON

Unafraid to get her hands dirty while on the hunt for a scoop, Vicki once lashed out at a would-be mugger, holding a taser to his face in order to get information from the hardened criminal.

Vicki Vale is one of the *Gotham Gazette*'s most respected reporters. While she's usually particular about her sources and their credibility, she was once manipulated by former police lieutenant Jason Bard to cast him as a hero in the eyes of Gotham City's public. While her articles landed her a promotion, it took a lot of apologising from Bard to win back her trust.

"It's insane...but not impossible."

Vicki Vale has several ethical coworkers at the *Gotham Gazette*, including crime editor Warren Stacey.

MAYOR SEBASTIAN HADY

VITAL STATS

Full Name: Sebastian Hady

Occupation: Mayor of Gotham City

Height: 1.68 m

Weight: 91.5 kg

Base: Gotham City

Allies: G.C.P.D., the Penguin, Carmine Falcone

Foes: James Gordon, Batman, Batman, Inc.

POWERS AND ABILITIES

Wealthy connections; control over Gotham City's police department; persuasive and influential networker.

MONEY ON HIS MIND

With a mind for money, Mayor Hady is quick to act in his own selfish interests. He once made a deal with Caldwell Technologies, not realising their CEO was a super-villain known as Wrath.

Gotham City is a corrupt metropolis, so it only follows that its leader, Mayor Sebastian Hady, is an unethical and unapologetic individual. Hady originally ran for mayor in the year Batman first began to operate in Gotham City. These days, Hady doesn't shy away from working hand in hand with organised criminals, including the Penguin.

Puts on a phony demeanour to appear likeable

Has gained weight since his campaign years

Well-dressed to look the part

"Batman is no longer welcome in Gotham City."

DR LESLIE THOMPKINS

VITAL STATS

Full Name: Dr Leslie Thompkins

Occupation: Medical doctor

Height: 1.70 m

Weight: 59 kg

Base: Gotham City

Allies: Batman and Bruce Wayne, the Batman Family, Catwoman

Foes: The Fist of Cain cult

POWERS AND ABILITIES

Skilled and knowledgeable doctor and surgeon; compassionate personality; opinionated with strong pacifist views; commands loyalty and respect; well-travelled and experienced.

ADOPTING STRAYS

With a passion for helping wayward youth, Dr Leslie Thompkins helped Catwoman years ago. She also helped a young Jason Todd, even after the young boy tried to steal from her clinic.

Dr Leslie Thompkins was there for Bruce Wayne the night his parents were murdered. She comforted him, and built a trust that would last into his career as Batman. One night, when he was badly injured, Batman came to Dr Thompkins at her clinic, and she discovered his alter ego. Since then, she has helped Batman, even if she sometimes disagrees with his methods.

"But you have to keep believing."

Leslie took an interest in student Duke Thomas's life after his parents went missing, and helped place him in a few different foster homes.

THE HUNTRESS

HERO

VITAL STATS

Real Name: Helena Bertinelli

Occupation: Head of Spyral, Headmistress at finishing school

Height: 1.80 m

Weight: 59 kg

Base: Saint Hadrian's Finishing School for Girls, England

Allies: Dick Grayson, the Hood, Agent 1

Foes: Mr Minos

POWERS AND ABILITIES

Highly skilled martial artist and fighter; expert at espionage and natural leader.

LOVE BIRDS?

Dick Grayson and Helena Bertinelli quickly became close allies in the field. They have learnt to trust each other in life-and-death situations, and it is becoming apparent that the two may want more than a professional partnership.

Helena Bertinelli is the reason Dick Grayson is working for the spy agency known as Spyral. Having vouched for the new recruit to the then head of the agency, Mr Minos, Helena became partners with Grayson in his new role as Agent 37. However, when Helena discovered how corrupt Minos was, she put an arrow through him in order to protect her agency's secrets.

Equipped with mind-influencing "hypnos"

Has face-altering identity protection implants

Expert crossbow sharp shooter

"From now on...I am Spyral."

SPYRAL

VITAL STATS

Team Name: Spyral
Base: Saint Hadrian's Finishing School, England
Allies: Network of secret agents
Foes: Batman, Dick Grayson, Batman, Inc.

Notable Members: Dick Grayson, the Huntress, Dr Dedalus, El Gaucho, The Hood, Mr Minos, Frau Netz, Dr Poppy Ashemore, Tiger

WHO WATCHES THE WATCHMEN?

During his time as the head of Spyral, Mr Minos kept tabs on all the world's superhumans, aided by one of his top scientists, and the daughter of Dr Dedalus, Frau Netz.

Originally founded by Nazi scientist Otto Netz (Dr Dedalus), Spyral is a clandestine agency that was led for many years by the enigmatic Mr Minos, with the goal of gathering information on the superhuman community. When the corrupt nature of Minos's mission was revealed, he was dethroned by agent Helena Bertinelli who took over as head of the organisation.

"Power cannot be masked."

Helena Bertinelli works with Dick Grayson as Agent 37, but doesn't realise that he has been secretly supplying Spyral information to Batman.

AMADEUS ARKHAM

VITAL STATS

Full Name: Amadeus Arkham

Occupation: Doctor of psychology

Height: 1.78 m

Weight: 76.5 kg

Base: Gotham City

Allies: Jonah Hex, Alan and Catherine Wayne

Foes: The Court of Owls, Religion of Crime

POWERS AND ABILITIES

Highly trained psychologist; extremely intelligent; many connections in Gotham City's high society.

A MAN OF LETTERS

Dr Amadeus Arkham kept many journals that detailed his own history and, later, his descent into madness. While he was the founder of Arkham Asylum, he would also end up as one of its disturbed patients.

A prominent doctor in Gotham City in 1880, Amadeus Arkham worked directly with infamous bounty hunter, Jonah Hex, when a serial killer went on a terrifying spree through the city. Amadeus later transformed his large family estate into Arkham Asylum, the notorious home away from home of such modern day villains as the Joker, Two-Face, and Clayface.

"...my interest lies in the inner workings of the mind."

Amadeus Arkham and Jonah Hex went on many missions together. Jonah was annoyed by Amadeus at first, but he grew to respect him.

JEREMIAH ARKHAM

VITAL STATS

Full Name: Jeremiah Arkham

Occupation: Director of Arkham Asylum

Height: 1.80 m

Weight: 79 kg

Base: Gotham City

Allies: Aaron Cash, G.C.P.D., Jonah Hex

Foes: The Court of Owls, Arkham Asylum inmates

POWERS AND ABILITIES

Highly trained psychologist; extremely intelligent; many connections in Gotham City's political world.

A PATH TO HEALING

Although stern, Dr Jeremiah Arkham has not yet grown jaded from his position as the director of Arkham Asylum. He remains steadfast in the belief that he can cure the many unstable patients who reside there.

Jeremiah Arkham's great-great grandfather was Amadeus Arkham, Arkham Asylum's founder. Despite a family history of insanity, Jeremiah dedicated his life to rehabilitating the city's worst offenders. Normally preferring a position on the sidelines, Arkham was forced on an adventure when a time-travelling Jonah Hex escaped custody and kidnapped him.

"...it sounds crazy, but...that's the Arkham family business."

Aaron Cash is another member of Arkham Asylum's staff. A hard-as-nails guard, he works tirelessly to keep the inmates in line.

ALAN WAYNE

VITAL STATS

Full Name: Alan Wayne

Occupation: Railroad tycoon, socialite and investor

Height: 1.80 m

Weight: 77.5 kg

Base: Gotham City

Allies: Catherine Wayne, Theodore Cobblepot, Edward Elliot, Cameron Kane, Amadeus Arkham

Foes: The Court of Owls, Nicholas and Bradley Gates

POWERS AND ABILITIES

Influential Gotham City socialite with powerful connections; extremely wealthy and intelligent.

DEATH OF THE FATHER

In 1922, Alan Wayne was held captive in the Court of Owls's underground labyrinth. When he emerged from the sewers, he ran straight into the arms of police officers before being killed by a Talon assassin.

Alan Wayne was the son of Judge Solomon Wayne, one of Gotham City's founders. Solomon had hired architect Cyrus Pinkney to build the city's first tall buildings and now Alan wanted to build even more. He hired architect brothers Nicholas and Bradley Gates to enhance the city's skyline, including building Wayne Tower. Alan was later killed by a Talon of the Court of Owls.

Alan, Bruce Wayne's great, great grandfather, and his wife Catherine took an active role in Gotham City's social issues.

"They're...coming for me!"

JASON BARD

VITAL STATS

Full Name: Jason Bard
Occupation: Former G.C.P.D. commissinner
Height: 1.83 m
Weight: 79 kg
Base: Gotham City
Allies: Hush, Vicki Vale, James Gordon
Foes: Mayor Sebastian Hady, Carmine Falcone, Batman

POWERS AND ABILITIES

Well-trained and highly intelligent police officer; finely-honed detective skills; connections to *Gotham Gazette* as well as to some of the worst criminals in Gotham City; keen strategist.

SETTING HIS SIGHTS ON BATMAN

Jason Bard received inaccurate information from Hush, which pointed to huge cover-ups perpetrated by Wayne Enterprises and Batman. Bard set out on a mission to reveal the "truth" and expose Batman.

Jason Bard was a Detroit police officer until his partner was killed in a battle with a vigilante who was imitating Batman. That night, Bard — furious at the real Batman — was approached by Batman's long-time foe, Hush. Hush used his connections to place Bard in the G.C.P.D., where he rose through the ranks to the position of commissioner.

"And that's how you take down a vigilante."

Batman has always respected Bard as a top detective. After many confrontations with Batman, Bard discovered the error of his ways.

GOTHAM ACADEMY STUDENTS

NEUTRAL

VITAL STATS

Student body includes:

Olive Silverlock,

Mia "Maps" Mizoguchi,

Kyle Mizoguchi,

Pomeline Fritch,

Colton Rivera,

Eric Jorgensen,

Tristan Grey,

Damian Wayne (expelled)

THE DETECTIVE CLUB

Olive Silverlock, her friend "Maps" Mizoguchi and Maps's brother Kyle are three of Gotham Academy's shining stars. Together they formed a Detective Club that investigates some of the strange happenings around campus.

One of Gotham City's most influential private schools, Gotham Academy boasts some impressive alumni. Bruce Wayne himself spent some time there as a student. These days, the school has a varied student body, including a young man cursed with the Langstrom Man-Bat virus, Tristan Grey, and Olive Silverlock, a teen who has the ability to produce and control fire.

"Every stone in these old walls has a story."

Olive is haunted by the fact that her late mother spent time in Arkham Asylum. But regardless, she makes friends, including youthful Maps.

GOTHAM ACADEMY FACULTY

VITAL STATS

Faculty includes:

Headmaster
"Hammerhead" Hammer,

Professor Isla MacPherson,

Professor Hugo Strange,

Dr Kirk Langstrom,

Coach Humphreys,

Mr Scarlett,

"Aunt" Harriet,

Mr Trent,

Professor Achilles Milo
(former teacher)

THE CUSTODIAN
Gotham Academy is steeped in legends, one of which is the story of the Custodian, a mysterious hero who stalks the campus grounds, fighting off threats. In reality, the Custodian is really Headmaster Hammer protecting his students.

Professor Isla MacPherson

Gotham Academy is a prestigious boarding school that has attracted expert teachers from many different walks of life. There are science classes taught by the Man-Bat, Dr Kirk Langstrom and Professor Milo. Another Professor, Hugo Strange, serves as the school's counsellor and there's "Bookworm" Mr Scarlett, as well as kindly "Aunt" Harriet.

Mr Scarlett, the school "Bookworm"

"Welcome to Gotham Academy."

Headmaster "Hammerhead" Hammer

HALY'S CIRCUS

NEUTRAL

VITAL STATS

Group Name:
Haly's Circus

Base: Mobile

Allies: Dick
Grayson, the
Court of Owls

Foes: Tony Zucco,
the Joker

**Notable Former
Members:**
C.C. Haly,
Dick Grayson,
John Grayson, Mary
Grayson, Bryan Haly,
Raya Vestri, Talon (Calvin
Rose), Talon (William
Cobb), Strix, Saiko

GOTHAM CITY NO MORE

For years, Haly's Circus
made Gotham City a
staple on its tour route.
However, when two
members of its star
act, the Flying Graysons,
were killed by gangster
Tony Zucco, the circus
didn't return to the city
for almost five years.

From all appearances, Haly's Circus
seems like an innocent institution, a
touring group of performers with an
extensive history. But most customers
are unaware of the dark secret that
lurks beneath the surface. Decades
ago, the nefarious Court of Owls
made a deal with Haly's to recruit the
circus's best and brightest stars to
serve as the Court's Talon assassins.

*"Ladies and gentlemen...the star
of Haly's Circus...Dick Grayson!"*

A star member of the Flying Graysons trapeze
act, Dick was a prime target for the Court of
Owls, but he managed to escape life as a Talon.

BARBARA KEAN GORDON

VITAL STATS

Full Name: Barbara Kean Gordon

Occupation: Unknown

Height: 1.70 m

Weight: 66 kg

Base: Unknown coast, formerly Gotham City

Allies: Batgirl, James Gordon

Foes: James Gordon, Jr, the Joker

POWERS AND ABILITIES

Intelligent but troubled; excellent baker.

BUILDING BRIDGES

It took a while before Barbara Kean Gordon could earn the forgiveness of her daughter. But after Barbara Gordon discovered why her mother really left, she let her mum back into her life.

Barbara Kean Gordon left her husband, James Gordon, and their two children, Barbara Gordon and James Gordon, Jr, after James, Jr killed the family cat, and threatened his sister, too. Although James, Jr was just a child, his mother believed his threats. Years later she returned and attempted to rekindle a relationship with her daughter, who had become Batgirl.

"Don't you recognise me, Barbara? I'm your mother."

Barbara Kean Gordon confronted her son upon her return to Gotham City. She wounded him and watched her daughter, Batgirl, defeat him.

JULIE MADISON

VITAL STATS

Full Name: Julie Madison

Occupation: Instructor at Lucius Fox Centre for Gotham Youth

Height: 1.63 m

Weight: 54 kg

Base: Gotham City

Allies: Bruce Wayne, Lucius Fox

Foe: Mr Bloom

POWERS AND ABILITIES

Extremely intelligent, witty, and creative; powerful connections in Gotham City.

A NEW START

With no memory of being Batman, Bruce Wayne is content in his life with Julie. Working together at the Lucius Fox Centre for Gotham Youth, Wayne and Julie are visited by James Gordon, who has taken on the role of Batman.

Julie Madison was one of Bruce Wayne's first girlfriends. Dating back in their school years, they formed a strong bond that soon faded due to Bruce's focus on his mission and his obsession with his parents' death. When Batman was presumed dead and James Gordon took up his duties, Julie returned to Bruce's life, and they rekindled their old flame.

Bruce hated having to choose between Julie and his life as Batman. When he made his choice, Alfred had to tell Julie that Bruce was spoken for.

"It's okay. Come on, let's go home."

HOLLY ROBINSON

VITAL STATS

Full Name: Holly Robinson
Occupation: Former Hero
Height: 1.61 m
Weight: 52 kg
Base: Mobile
Allies: Catwoman, Slam Bradley, Harley Quinn
Foes: Black Mask, Film Freak

POWERS AND ABILITIES

Extremely fit and agile; adept hand-to-hand combatant with an emphasis on boxing techniques; proficient in the use of Catwoman's equipment.

CATWOMAN IN TRAINING

Holly Robinson feels a true love for Gotham City's East End, and felt the need to protect it during Catwoman's brief retirement. Unfortunately, she never quite settled into the demanding role.

Holly Robinson **grew up** in a troubled home, and eventually ran away to try living on her own in Gotham City's East End. With a rough road ahead of her, Holly was fortunate enough to befriend Selina Kyle, and learnt of Selina's fledgling career as the cat burglar Catwoman. Holly even briefly donned the Catwoman costume herself when Selina temporarily retired.

Quick-witted and fast to react to danger

Slight build enables stealth

Thin frame from her life living on the streets

"Gee, it truly is a glamorous profession!"

THE JUSTICE LEAGUE

VITAL STATS

Team Name: The Justice League

Base: Watchtower satellite in Earth's orbit

Allies: Black Lightning, the Teen Titans, Black Canary

Foes: Darkseid, Anti-Monitor, the Crime Syndicate

Members:
Batman, Superman, Wonder Woman, Aquaman, Green Lantern (Hal Jordan), the Flash, Cyborg, Shazam, Power Ring, Martian Manhunter (former), Firestorm (former), Element Woman (former), Atomica (traitor), Lex Luthor, Captain Cold

NEW PARTNERSHIPS

It took some time for the founding Justice League members to trust one another. Some members, like Batman and Superman, began working together as partners outside of their Justice League missions.

The Justice League first formed when the other-dimensional tyrant Darkseid attempted to conquer Earth. Batman, Wonder Woman, Superman, Green Lantern, Cyborg, Aquaman and the Flash successfully fought back, and decided to team up to battle other large-scale threats. Their roster has changed a few times, but they remain unwavering in their mission.

"You can call us... the Super Seven!"

The Justice League inducted "reformed" villains, Lex Luthor and Captain Cold, into their ranks after Luthor helped defeat the Crime Syndicate.

SUPERMAN

VITAL STATS

Real Name: Clark Kent, Kal-El

Occupation: Hero, reporter

Height: 1.91 m

Weight: 106.5 kg

Base: Metropolis

Allies: The Justice League, Steel, Supergirl, Superboy

Foes: Lex Luthor, Doomsday, Parasite, Darkseid

POWERS AND ABILITIES

Super-strength; super-speed; superhuman reflexes, senses, durability and endurance; flight; heat vision; X-ray vision; freeze breath; solar flare; extremely intelligent; access to advanced Kryptonian technology; powers derived from Earth's yellow sun.

BREAK THE CHAINS
Superman is a match for any hero or villain. Green Lantern quickly learnt this fact during the formation of the Justice League, when he tried and failed to restrain the Man of Steel with green energy constructs.

Baby Kal-El was rocketed to Earth when his planet, Krypton, exploded. Discovered by the Kent family, the infant was renamed Clark. As he matured, Clark discovered that Earth's yellow sun gave him awesome abilities. He soon put these powers to use in order to protect his adopted city of Metropolis as the ultimate Super Hero, Superman.

Kryptonian costume was found on alien conqueror Brainiac's ship

S-Shield is the symbol of his Kryptonian family

Superman's cape is indestructible

"Treat people right or expect a visit from me."

CLARK KENT

VITAL STATS

Full Name: Clark Kent, Kal-El

Occupation: Hero, reporter

Height: 1.91 m

Weight: 106.5 kg

Base: Metropolis

Allies: Lois Lane, Jimmy Olsen, Perry White, Bruce Wayne

Foes: Lex Luthor, Doomsday, Parasite, Darkseid

POWERS AND ABILITIES

Extremely intelligent; access to contacts from the world of journalism; mild-mannered persona created to deflect attention; excellent investigative skills.

SEEKER OF TRUTH

Beginning his career at the *Daily Star*, Clark Kent wrote intriguing and fearless exposés. He befriended the wealthy Jimmy Olsen in the process, as well as his longtime crush, another ace reporter, Lois Lane.

Everybody knows that Clark Kent grew up in Smallville, Kansas, and was raised by Jonathan and Martha Kent. But for years, Clark hid the fact that he is an alien from the distant planet Krypton. Clark was sent to Earth by his birth parents, Jor-El and Lara, when his planet was destroyed. Clark dedicates his career to truth as a reporter for the *Daily Planet*.

"I've waited my whole life for this."

Since most people don't think Superman has time for a secret life, his idea of hiding in plain sight, behind a pair of glasses, works perfectly.

SUPERGIRL

VITAL STATS

Real Name: Kara Zor-El
Occupation: Hero
Height: .65 m
Weight: 54 kg
Base: Mobile
Allies: Superman, Superboy, the Justice League United, Steel
Foes: Jochi, Silver Banshee, H'el

POWERS AND ABILITIES

Super-strength; super-speed; superhuman reflexes, durability, senses and endurance; flight; heat vision; freeze breath; X-ray vision; access to advanced Kryptonian technology; power derived from Earth's yellow sun.

WORLD'S FINEST

In order to defeat the threat of the alien Jochi, Superman and Batman had to pick two champion allies to compete in Warworld's deadly gladiatorial arena. Superman chose Steel and Supergirl and Batman chose Red Hood and Batgirl.

Kara Zor-El came from a prestigious family who lived in Argo City, one of the biggest metropolises on planet Krypton. Her scientist father, Zor-El, was Jor-El's brother. As Jor-El built a rocket ship to allow his baby Kal-El to escape Krypton's destruction, Zor-El created an escape pod for his daughter. Kara found her way to Earth and adopted the guise of Supergirl.

Like Clark Kent, she has freeze breath

Wears the El family S-Shield

Can fly at high speeds

"You have to trust me to find my own way."

WONDER WOMAN

VITAL STATS

Real Name: Diana
Occupation: Hero, queen,
God of War
Height: 1.83 m
Weight: 75 kg
Base: Themyscira
Allies: Superman, Orion,
the Justice League
Foes: Cheetah, Circe,
the First Born

POWERS AND ABILITIES

Godly blood grants her
super-strength, endurance
and agility; power of flight;
Bracelets of Victory can
deflect bullets; expert fighter
and strategist; Lasso of
Truth forces others to tell
the truth; extremely wise
and empathetic.

HEAR HER ROAR

Wonder Woman has
occasionally changed her
armour, but always retains
the "star" iconography
that represents her family
lineage. An emissary of
peace, she is also a true
warrior at heart.

Diana is the daughter of the god Zeus
and Hippolyta, the ruler of Themyscira,
an island of female warriors called the
Amazons. Diana grew up a princess
completely isolated from the rest of the
world. When a pilot named Steve Trevor
crashed on Themyscira, Diana learnt of
the outside world and soon travelled there
as her people's representative and a true
Super Hero – Wonder Woman.

*"It's a big, strange and
wondrous universe."*

Armour
forged by god
Hephaestus

Tiara a sign of
regal lineage

Bracelets of
Victory can
produce
blades

Flexible armour
for ease of
movement

Lasso can be
used to attack
or defend

AQUAMAN

VITAL STATS

Real Name:
Arthur Curry
Occupation: Hero, king
of Atlantis
Height: 1.85 m
Weight: 147.5 kg
Base: Atlantis
Allies: Mera, the Justice
League, the Others
Foes: Black Manta, Ocean
Master, the Trench

POWERS AND ABILITIES

Can breathe underwater;
can communicate with and
control sea life; ruler of
underwater kingdom of
Atlantis; super-strength;
trained fighter and natural
leader; swims incredibly fast.

FISH OUT OF WATER

Batman and Aquaman have fought
side-by-side on many missions as part
of the Justice League. The two have
also teamed up as partners on occasion,
including the time they battled Rā's al
Ghūl on a remote island in the Pacific.

Body can bear
pressures of
the deep

Blond hair rare
in Atlantis

Carries
trident to
use as
weapon

Wears
scale-like
uniform

Arthur Curry was born to a
lighthouse keeper and an Atlantean
queen, and raised on land when his
mother returned to the sea. Thanks
to his ability to breathe underwater
and communicate with sea life, Arthur
became known as Aquaman when he
was a young man. The rightful king of
Atlantis, he uses his abilities to fight
for creatures on land and in the ocean.

*"So who's in charge here?
I vote me."*

GREEN LANTERN

VITAL STATS

Real Name: Harold (Hal) Jordan

Occupation: Hero

Height: 1.88 m

Weight: 84 kg

Base: Mobile, Coast City

Allies: The Justice League, Green Lantern Corps

Foes: Sinestro, Red Lanterns, Black Hand

POWERS AND ABILITIES

Expert pilot; natural leader; Green Lantern ring can create physical manifestations of anything its user imagines; it also allows for flight, force fields and space travel, and can impart encyclopedic knowledge to its wearer.

EMERALD KNIGHT

Green Lantern and Batman first met during Darkseid's invasion of the Earth. Hal Jordan was surprised to learn that the Dark Knight possessed no special powers, and was simply Bruce Wayne in an armoured uniform.

Ring creates Hal's mask and uniform

Responsible for protecting space sector 2814

Green power ring creates anything Hal can imagine

As a child, Hal Jordan idolised his pilot father, who died in a plane crash. Hal grew up to be just like his dad, overcoming his fear of flying and finding work at Ferris Airlines. When Abin Sur, a member of the galactic peacekeepers known as the Green Lanterns, crashed his spaceship on Earth, his magical ring chose Hal to replace Abin Sur as the newest member of the Green Lanterns.

"You're not just some guy in a bat costume, are you?"

GREEN LANTERN

VITAL STATS

Real Name: John Stewart

Occupation: Hero

Height: 1.85 m

Weight: 05 kg

Base: Mobile

Allies: Green Lantern Corps, Hal Jordan, Kilowog

Foes: Red Lantern Corps, Larfleeze, Sinestro Corps

POWERS AND ABILITIES

Expert architect; military training; natural leader; Green Lantern ring can create physical manifestations of anything its user imagines; it also allows for flight, force fields and space travel, and can impart encyclopedic knowledge to its wearer.

THE LOGICAL LANTERN

John Stewart is a military man and a former architect. As such, he thinks logically and precisely. While some of his fellow Green Lanterns may conjure fanciful objects with their rings, John keeps his constructs efficient.

The son of a political activist, John Stewart grew up learning to fight for what's right — peacefully. He left home in Detroit, Michigan, to join the Marines, and helped with the relief effort during the superstorm that caused Gotham City's blackout. But after falling out with his superiors, John was honourably discharged, only to be enlisted in a greater army, the Green Lantern Corps.

"This is the end of the road...just not for me."

As a member of the intergalactic peacekeeping force, the Green Lantern Corps, John Stewart has finally found his purpose in life.

CYBORG

VITAL STATS

Real Name: Victor Stone
Occupation: Hero, scientist
Height: 1.96 m
Weight: 174.5 kg
Base: Detroit, Michigan
Allies: The Justice League, the Metal Men, S.T.A.R. Labs
Foes: Grid, the Crime Syndicate, Darkseid

POWERS AND ABILITIES

Cybernetic body allows for enhanced endurance, durability, agility, speed and strength; can tap into world grid allowing internet access; computer and robotics expert; adept hacker; naturally athletic and intelligent; hi-tech weapons include white-noise blaster.

WORK IN PROGRESS

Cyborg is a founder of the Justice League, and was its youngest member until Shazam joined. After being attacked by the artificial life form known as Grid, Victor completely upgraded his cybernetic body.

A star football player in high school, Victor Stone was at odds with his father, who wanted Vic to pursue education over athletics. When Darkseid invaded Earth, Vic was mortally wounded, saved only when his father subjected him to an experimental cybernetic bonding process, turning him into a cyborg. Vic put his advanced artificial body to use, becoming a hero.

"What am I?"

Can access internet with a mere thought

Robotic body is incredibly durable

Favours white noise blasts of energy

THE FLASH

VITAL STATS

Real Name: Barry Allen

Occupation: Hero, forensic scientist

Height: 1.80 m

Weight: 81 kg

Base: Central City

Allies: The Justice League, Green Lantern, Iris West

Foes: Captain Cold, Mirror Master, Heatwave, Captain Boomerang

POWERS AND ABILITIES

Draws super-speed powers from an extradimensional Speed Force energy; extremely intelligent; well-versed in police procedure and detection; skilled crime scene investigator.

SPEED BUMPS

The Flash has gathered his own Rogues Gallery over the years, from villains like Heatwave, to murderers like the Keystone Killer. As the Flash, and as a crime scene investigator, he does his best to protect his city.

When Barry Allen was a boy, his mother died, and his father was arrested as the culprit. Desperate to get to the truth, Barry studied forensics, and later became a criminologist for the police. One night, a bolt of lightning struck a shelf of chemicals, splashing them onto Allen, giving him the power to move at fantastic speeds as the Flash.

"No matter what — I'll never stop chasing the truth."

Designed his own flame-coloured costume

Costume can shrink small enough to fit inside a ring

Speed causes lightning to trail off behind him

GREEN ARROW

VITAL STATS

Real Name: Oliver Queen

Occupation: Hero, head of the Queen Foundation

Height: 1.80 m

Weight: 84 kg

Base: Seattle, Washington

Allies: The Justice League of America, Katana, Arsenal, Batman

Foes: Count Vertigo, Richard Dragon II, the Clock King

POWERS AND ABILITIES

Expert archer with variety of arrows; skilled hand-to-hand combatant and martial artist.

TAKING AIM

During his crime-fighting career, Green Arrow has amassed his own Rogues Gallery, from the team of Midas and Blood Rose, to the master martial artist Richard Dragon and the gang leader, the Clock King.

Heir to the Queen fortune, Oliver Queen lived a life of excess. Despite being trained from an early age in the art of the bow and arrow by his father, Robert, Oliver didn't embrace the skill until he was stranded on a deserted island for three years. Oliver eventually escaped from the island, and reemerged in Seattle a changed man, fighting criminals as the hero Green Arrow.

"I won't let anyone else get hurt in this city because of me."

Quiver filled with array of trick arrows

Armoured suit helps protect from damage

Belt contains small crime-fighting tools

Bow also used as handle for zip lines

Shins and forearms have added armour

MARTIAN MANHUNTER

VITAL STATS

Real Name: J'onn J'onzz
Occupation: Hero
Height: 2 m
Weight: 113 kg
Base: Mobile
Allies: The Justice League of America, the Justice League, Stormwatch, the Justice League United
Foes: The Crime Syndicate, the Secret Society

POWERS AND ABILITIES

Super-strength; super-speed; superhuman agility and endurance; invisibility; shape-shifting powers; flight; telepathy; Martian vision; able to pass through solid objects; highly intelligent and determined; natural leader.

SUPER-MANHUNTER

The Martian Manhunter is one of the most powerful Super Heroes. Possessing most of the abilities of Superman, J'onn's shape-shifting, telepathy and invisibility powers give him a huge advantage in any fight.

Can communicate with others by thought

Green skin a sign of Martian heritage

Costume can shape-shift with his flesh

Body can pass through solid objects

The people of Mars lived a connected life, communicating with each other through their thoughts. When J'onn J'onzz became their leader, he journeyed to another world to experience the feeling of being alone. When he returned he found Mars aflame. Believing he was the planet's sole survivor, he travelled to Earth to use his powers for good as the Martian Manhunter.

"My friends call me J'onn..."

LEX LUTHOR

VITAL STATS

Full Name: Lex Luthor

Occupation: CEO of LexCorp, criminal

Height: 1.88 m

Weight: 95 kg

Base: Metropolis

Allies: Captain Cold, the Justice League, Mercy Graves, Brainiac

Foes: Superman, the Crime Syndicate, Batman

POWERS AND ABILITIES

Near unparalleled intellect; armoured flight suit equipped with hi-tech weaponry and defences; suit grants him superhuman strength and speed.

INJUSTICE FOR ALL

After convincing the world he was a true hero by playing a major part in the defeat of the Crime Syndicate, Lex Luthor rallied public support to become a member of the Justice League.

Lex Luthor first met Superman whilst working with the United States government and the alien entity known as Brainiac. Wishing to be mankind's saviour against the alien threat Superman presented, he helped capture and experiment on the Kryptonian hero but Superman escaped. Luthor has maintained a vendetta against Superman ever since.

"I'm a changed man, Superman."

Genius-level intellect and business savvy

Clothes suit his luxurious lifestyle

Dresses in business attire, when not in hero costume

BLACK LIGHTNING

VITAL STATS

Real Name: Jefferson Pierce
Occupation: Hero,
high school teacher
Height: 1.85 m
Weight: 91 kg
Base: Los Angeles,
California
Allies: Batman, Blue Devil,
the Justice League,
Foe: Tobias Whale

POWERS AND ABILITIES

Can generate black
electricity from his own
body; Olympic-level athlete;
natural leader; excellent
teacher with a very
intelligent mind.

BLACK AND BLUE

Black Lightning has been
known to team with the
magical hero Blue Devil.
Before the two were
Super Hero partners,
they were old high school
friends who played on
the same football team.

Jefferson Pierce's father is a reporter
who instilled a strong sense of right
and wrong in his son. Jefferson grew
up to become an Olympic gold medalist
in track and field, and later evolved
into the electricity-powered hero Black
Lightning. He formed a partnership
with Blue Devil and was even recruited
by Batman and the Justice League,
but chose not to become a member.

*"Never lose your focus
in a fight!"*

Visor hides
identity and
protects eyes

Costume
can generate
electricity too

Altered costume
to include gold
design

THE OUTSIDERS

VITAL STATS

Team Name: The Outsiders

Base: Gotham City

Allies: Batman, Batman, Inc., Alfred Pennyworth

Foes: Mr Freeze, Clayface, Leviathan, Masters of Disaster

Notable Members:
Geo-Force, Halo, Katana, Metamorpho, Black Lightning, Looker, Red Robin, Freight Train, Owlman (Roy Raymond, Jr)

OUTSIDE HELP
When Batman was sent time travelling by the villain Darkseid, Alfred Pennyworth decided to unite his allies, the Outsiders, into a new team to pick up where the Dark Knight left off.

The team of Super Heroes called the Outsiders has shared a long history with Batman and his allies. United some time ago as Batman's personal strike force to go on missions the Justice League wouldn't touch, the Outsiders have proved themselves devoutly loyal to the Dark Knight, repeatedly putting their lives on the line, even against the evil forces of Leviathan.

"We're a low maintenance crowd."

When uniting against the forces of Leviathan, Batman teamed the Outsiders with their new leader and his former partner, Red Robin.

KATANA

VITAL STATS

Real Name: Tatsu Toro
Occupation: Hero, assassin
Height: 1.67 m
Weight: 43.5 kg
Base: Japantown, San Francisco, California
Allies: The Birds of Prey, the Justice League of America, Batman
Foes: The Creeper, Coil, Killer Croc

POWERS AND ABILITIES

Skilled martial artist with expertise in swordsmanship; communicates with deceased inhabitants of her sword.

OUTSIDER ON THE INSIDE

Katana is often at odds with the Sword Clan crime family, including its deadly member Coil. She allied herself briefly with the Swords, but was never an official member as she was with the Justice League of America and the Birds of Prey.

Tatsu Toro was torn between her husband, Maseo Yamashiro, and his brother, Takeo, a martial artist. During a fight between them, Tatsu stepped in, accidentally killing Maseo and trapping his soul in the Soultaker sword. Tatsu dedicated her life to fighting and swordsmanship as Katana, maintaining a relationship with Maseo's trapped soul.

"...I am not here to make friends."

Soultaker sword traps the souls of its victims

Wears colours of Japan's flag on her mask

Armoured suit provides full-body protection

Armoured patch protects against swords

Lightweight suit worn under casual clothing

METAMORPHO

VITAL STATS

Real Name: Rex Mason
Occupation: Hero, adventurer
Height: 1.85 m
Weight: 91 kg
Base: Haneyville
Allies: Batman, Inc., the Outsiders, Batman, Sapphire Stagg
Foes: Simon Stagg, Leviathan, Java

POWERS AND ABILITIES

Can transform his body into any element or mix of elements found in the human body; brave explorer with loyal heart; superhuman recovery and endurance; knowledge of ancient artefacts.

CURSE THE ELEMENTS

Despite possessing amazing powers that enable him to turn himself as hard as steel or as untouchable as a gas, Metamorpho simply wants to return to human form and continue his life with Sapphire Stagg.

An adventurer who loved a challenge, Rex Mason was in love with Sapphire Stagg, daughter of the wealthy and corrupt Simon Stagg. While exploring an ancient pyramid, Rex was betrayed by Stagg's henchman and exposed to a meteor that changed him into Metamorpho, the Element Man. He put his powers to good use as a member of Batman's Outsiders team.

Master of simultaneous transformations

Face and body stuck in bizarre colours

Can transform entire body or small sections

"Always one step a — head."

GEO-FORCE

VITAL STATS

Real Name: Brion Markov

Occupation: Ruler of Markovia

Height: 1.90 m

Weight: 95 kg

Base: Markovia

Allies: The Outsiders, Batman, Terra

Foes: Masters of Disaster, Clayface, Baron Bedlam

POWERS AND ABILITIES

Projects lava blasts from hands; can increase or decrease gravity on himself or others; combines lava blast and gravity powers to propel himself via flight; superhuman strength, endurance and durability; able to manipulate earth and rock.

MOVER AND SHAKER

Due to the evil schemes of the villain Deathstroke, Geo-Force gained the ability of a so-called "earth-mover". This means he is able to control and manipulate rocks and dirt, abilities that complement his gravity powers.

The Prince of the Eastern European nation of Markovia, Brion Markov had a bright future ahead of him. A keen patriot, he volunteered himself for an experiment that gave him earth-themed powers. He adopted the identity of Geo-Force and became a founding member of the Outsiders. He is a loyal ally of the Dark Knight when not serving his country as its ruler.

"...isn't it time for evil to be punished?"

Brion became ruler of Markovia after the death of his brother. He now has the ability to protect his people from the throne and on the battlefield.

HALO

VITAL STATS

Real Name: Gabrielle Doe

Occupation: Hero

Height: 1.70 m

Weight: 54 kg

Base: Mobile

Allies: The Outsiders, Batman, Inc., Batman

Foes: Leviathan, Talia al Ghūl, Syonide II

POWERS AND ABILITIES

Controls and manipulates visible energy, called an aura: red aura generates heat; orange aura projects force blasts; yellow aura generates light; green aura keeps things still; blue distortion aura causes illusions; indigo aura is a tractor beam; all auras enable flight and space travel.

GROWING PAINS
As a member of the Outsiders, Halo matured from a naïve girl to a strong and independent young woman, often guided by the woman she saw as a mother figure, Katana.

Before Batman gave her the name Halo, the woman who would adopt the name of Gabrielle Doe wasn't a woman at all, but an Aurakle, a cosmic being from a race older than time itself. Curious about human life, this Aurakle reached out to a dying girl, Violet Harper, and found herself trapped in the girl's human form. She forgot her own past for a time and became Halo.

"Halo here. Everything's okay."

Halo's green aura is her stasis aura. It can freeze any living thing or chemical reaction in place, but it doesn't work on machines or affect gravity.

SHAZAM!

VITAL STATS

Real Name: Billy Batson

Occupation: Hero, student

Height: 1.85 m

Weight: 88.5 kg

Base: Philadelphia

Allies: The Justice League, Freddy Freeman

Foes: Black Adam, Mazahs, Dr Sivana, Mr Mind

POWERS AND ABILITIES

Superhuman wisdom, courage, strength, endurance, agility, speed, senses and durability; flight; ability to call down magic lightning; can transform from teen to adult by saying the magic word, "Shazam!"

BLACK MAGIC

With one word, "Shazam!", teenager Billy Batson is transformed into a mystically-powered adult, controlling the power of living lightning. His abilities came in handy when forced to combat his would-be usurper, Black Adam.

Can share magic with others if he so chooses

Magic lightning bolt symbol constantly glows

Costume appears when he transforms

An orphan, 15-year-old Billy Batson was taken in by the kindly Vasquez family. One night, the subway car Billy was riding in magically took him to the Rock of Eternity where he met an old wizard. The wizard turned him into the Super Hero Shazam! After facing down the threat of villain Black Adam, Shazam put his powers to good use by joining the Justice League.

"You picked the wrong person to push around."

THE JUSTICE LEAGUE OF AMERICA

VITAL STATS

Team Name: The Justice League of America

Base: A.R.G.U.S. headquarters, Washington, D.C.

Allies: The Justice League, Amanda Waller

Foes: The Secret Society, the Crime Syndicate

Members: Colonel Steve Trevor, Catwoman, Katana, Green Arrow, Hawkman, Stargirl, Martian Manhunter, Green Lantern Simon Baz, Vibe, Dr Light

BOXING MATCH
Shortly after the Justice League of America formed, they fought the original Justice League over a relic called Pandora's Box. What they didn't realise was that the box opened a portal to the nefarious dimension Earth-Three.

Worried that the Justice League did not operate under government control, the US government directed Amanda Waller to create an official US Super Hero team. Waller recruited Steve Trevor to lead the all-new Justice League of America. Ready to take down the original Justice League if required, the JLA was the country's first line of defence against superhuman threats.

"We introduce the JLA to the world tomorrow."

With the teen icon Stargirl a member, the team was welcomed onto the Super Hero scene by the masses.

THE TEEN TITANS

HEROES

VITAL STATS

Team Name: The Teen Titans

Base: New York City

Allies: The Batman Family, the Outlaws, S.T.A.R. Labs

Foes: Harvest, Trigon, Deathstroke

Members: Red Robin, Bunker, Beast Boy, Raven, Superboy, Wonder Girl (former), Power Girl (former), Kid Flash (former), Solstice (former), Skitter (former), Danny the Alley (former)

S.T.A.R.S OF THE SHOW
When there's trouble, call the Teen Titans. The latest incarnation of the team began working hand in hand with the scientifically advanced S.T.A.R. Labs and includes Beast Boy, Red Robin, Bunker and Raven.

When teen heroes were being captured by a villain called Harvest, Red Robin decided to recruit young metahumans and form a team of Super Heroes to combat the threat. He enlisted the help of Wonder Girl and other young heroes, including Kid Flash and Bunker. Together, they ended Harvest's reign of terror, and the team continues to fight injustice as the Teen Titans.

"Maybe we can do great things together."

Once an important member of the Teen Titans, Wonder Girl quit its ranks to lead a morally questionable team called the Elite.

THE OUTLAWS

VITAL STATS

Team Name: The Outlaws
Base: Unnamed, uncharted island
Allies: Batman, the Batman Family, Crux
Foes: Rā's al Ghūl, the Untitled, Suzie Su

Members:
Red Hood
Arsenal
Starfire

AN ATTACK ON CRIME
The Outlaws often chose to pursue figures from the world of organised crime. One such unlucky individual was the Hong Kong crime lord known as Suzie Su, who didn't survive their last encounter.

Green Arrow's former partner Arsenal was imprisoned in in the eastern nation of Qura. He was rescued by the Super Hero Red Hood and Starfire, an alien princess from the planet Tamaran. The three set up a base in Starfire's marooned starship, forming a team called the Outlaws. Starfire later quit, leaving Red Hood and Arsenal to form a partnership.

"We were friends, helping each other...we were outlaws!"

Starfire, aka Princess Koriand'r

Arsenal, aka Roy Harper

Red Hood, aka Jason Todd

RAGMAN

VITAL STATS

Real Name: Rory Regan
Occupation: Hero,
pawnshop owner
Height: 1.80 m
Weight: 75 kg
Base: Gotham City
Allies: Batwoman, the
Unknowns, Batman
Foe: Morgaine le Fey

POWERS AND ABILITIES

Wears suit of rags
composed of evil souls;
can absorb souls into
his suit in order to stop
corrupt individuals; granted
strengths and knowledge
of those imprisoned in his
rags; superhuman agility,
speed and strength;
can float on air currents.

RAGTIME

The mysterious Ragman has teamed
up with Batman in the past, and
became a staunch ally of Batwoman
as a fellow member of the Unknowns.
He was integral in the defeat of evil
sorceress Morgaine le Fey.

Constantly
struggling with
the evil souls
within his rags

Suit clothes
him when
he is needed

By day, the owner of the Rags 'n'
Tatters pawnshop in Gotham City,
Rory Regan does his best to help his
neighbours in tough times. By night,
he patrols the city in a mystical living
suit of rags that summons him when
he is needed. Rory's suit is actually
a cloth "golem" of sorts, created by
an ancient Council of Rabbis to
protect the Jewish people.

Rags surround
and speak
to him

Can be as light
as rags, to float
on wind

"I specialise in finding truths."

THE JOKER

VITAL STATS

Real Name: Unknown
Occupation: Criminal
Height: 1.96 m
Weight: 87 kg
Base: Gotham City
Allies: Harley Quinn,
the Joker's Daughter,
the Red Hood Gang
Foes: Batman, the Batman
Family, James Gordon

POWERS AND ABILITIES

Insanity causes unpredictable
behaviour; agile and a
relentless fighter; twisted
genius mind with expertise in
chemistry; brilliant strategist;
lacks moral code; employs
clown-themed weapons;
Venom gives his victims
permanent grins.

KILLER CLOWN FROM GOTHAM CITY

The Joker considers himself Batman's
arch-enemy, and is virtually obsessed
with the hero and his team. During his
career, he has temporarily paralysed
Batgirl and killed Jason Todd, and even
severed Alfred's hand.

While his true identity remains a
mystery, the Joker is believed to have
been the criminal known as Red Hood
One, the man in charge of the Red
Hood Gang. That chapter of his life
ended when Batman took down his
organisation and knocked the criminal
into a vat of chemicals. The Joker
survived, albeit with severely altered
features, including a damaged mind.

*"Just think of the great times
we've had...and smile!"*

Uses razor-
sharp playing
cards as
weapons

Hair dyed green
from chemical
exposure

Trademark
purple suit
with clashing
shirt and tie

Employs deadly
"jokes" like acid-
squirting flowers

HARLEY QUINN

VITAL STATS

Real Name: Dr Harleen Quinzel

Occupation: Criminal, landlord, roller derby participant

Height: 1.70 m

Weight: 52 kg

Base: Coney Island, Brooklyn, New York

Allies: The Joker, Suicide Squad, Poison Ivy, Scarecrow

Foes: Batman, the Batman Family

POWERS AND ABILITIES

Insanity causes unpredictability; agile and capable fighter; employs dozens of clown-themed weapons and lackeys; often uses giant hammer as a weapon.

LEFT HER HEART IN GOTHAM CITY

Putting Gotham City and her love affair with the Joker behind her, Harley Quinn moved to Coney Island and set up shop as a landlord, taking part in roller derbies.

Harley Quinn was a Gotham University graduate who began working at Arkham Asylum. To gain the inmates' trust, she dyed her hair two-toned and posed as a patient. The Joker saw through her ruse, and Harley found herself falling in love with him. They escaped Arkham, and the Joker threw her into a vat of chemicals to bleach her skin and cement their relationship.

"Oh, Mistah J..."

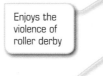

Enjoys the violence of roller derby

Adept at using trademark giant hammer

Skin bleached white thanks to the Joker

Not averse to using traditional guns

THE PENGUIN

VITAL STATS

Real Name: Oswald Chesterfield Cobblepot

Occupation: Crime boss, owner of the Iceberg Casino

Height: 1.57 m

Weight: 79 kg

Base: Gotham City

Allies: Lark, Catwoman, Mr Toxic, Hypnotic, Mr Combustible

Foes: Batman, the Batman Family, Black Canary

POWERS AND ABILITIES

Master strategist; brilliant criminal mind; employs a variety of trick umbrellas; major underworld connections.

OLD ENEMIES

Batman and the Penguin have a long history, going back to a time before either of them had adopted their animal-themed names. Batman often takes advantage of the Penguin's extensive criminal ties, scaring information out of the villain.

White gloves coordinate with the spats on his shoes

Physical features resemble a penguin

Weapons are concealed in his umbrellas

Agile and violent despite his size

Oswald Chesterfield Cobblepot hails from one of Gotham City's oldest and most influential families, albeit a corrupt one. Determined to climb to the top of the heap, Oswald continued his family's legacy, dealing in illegal weapons. Now known as the Penguin, he rose to power in Gotham City's underworld, becoming a feared crime boss and owner of the Iceberg Casino.

"Almost everything went according to plan, little birdie."

SCARECROW

VITAL STATS

Real Name: Dr Jonathan Crane

Occupation: Criminal, former psychiatrist and college professor

Height: 1.83 m

Weight: 63.5 kg

Base: Gotham City

Allies: The Secret Society, Professor Pyg, Merrymaker, Harley Quinn, Mr Freeze

Foes: Batman, the Batman Family

POWERS AND ABILITIES

Near genius intellect; brilliant chemist and psychiatrist; crafts fear gas that causes victims to live their worst nightmares.

KNIGHT TERRORS

Scarecrow is obsessed with fear, taking every opportunity to experiment on his favourite subject, Batman. Using his "fear toxin", he has forced the Dark Knight to relive his tragic past – but Batman triumphs over his inner demons.

As a boy, Jonathan Crane's father carried out twisted experiments that tested the emotion of fear. Despite this scary experience, Jonathan followed in his father's footsteps, studying fear as a professor at university. Eventually, his own cruel experiments led to him being fired, which was when he adopted the role of the deadly Scarecrow.

Fabric mask with sewn-up mouth

Costume rigged to dispense fear gas

Adopted the name Scarecrow after being compared to one

"I'm the bogeyman."

THE RIDDLER

VITAL STATS

Real Name: Edward Nygma
Occupation: Criminal, former Wayne Enterprises employee
Height: 1.85 m
Weight: 83 kg
Base: Gotham City
Allies: Arkham Rogues
Foes: Batman, the Batman Family

POWERS AND ABILITIES

Genius-level intellect; expert at creating riddles and death traps; computer and electronics whiz; not above cheating to win a fight.

RIDDLE ME THIS

Obsessed with riddles from a young age, the Riddler began his campaign of crime by taking Gotham City hostage. Not only did the villain shut off Gotham City's power, but he also would have obliterated the city entirely, if not for Batman's intervention.

Edward Nygma originally worked as an advisor for Bruce Wayne's uncle, Philip Kane, at Wayne Enterprises. Even more corrupt than his employer, Nygma met the young Bruce Wayne soon after Bruce's return to Gotham City, and challenged him with a series of riddles. Following a falling out with Kane, Nygma became the Riddler — one of Batman's trickiest opponents.

"It's not a mystery you're dealing with here. It's a riddle."

Bowler hat has replaced his old fedora

Trick cane loaded with remote technology

Trademark green suit

POISON IVY

VITAL STATS

Real Name; Pamela Lillian Isley

Occupation: Criminal, eco-terrorist

Height: 1.73 m

Weight: 52 kg

Base: Gotham City

Allies: Harley Quinn, Clayface, the Justice League United

Foes: Batman, the Batman Family, the Birds of Prey

POWERS AND ABILITIES

Controls and manipulates growth of plants; immune to toxins and poisons; produces pheromones that cause others to fall into her control; poisonous kiss; highly adept at botany and chemistry.

TANGLED IN IVY

Poison Ivy and Batman have clashed frequently, but they first butted heads when Isley worked briefly for Wayne Enterprises. She was fired for developing a mind-controlling pheromone that Bruce Wayne found immoral.

Can "speak" to plants and control them

Highly intelligent, with a mind for chemistry

Body changes with seasons like a true plant

Wears plant-based living costume

As a girl, Pamela Isley was adept at chemistry and developed a deadly toxin in her mother's garden that she could deliver to her enemies with a kiss. When she was accidentally doused with an experimental plant-based serum during a struggle in her lab, she gained the ability to communicate with nature. She soon set out to exploit that power as the eco-terrorist, Poison Ivy.

"Are you scared, little mammal?"

TWO-FACE

VITAL STATS

Real Name: Harvey Dent
Occupation: Criminal,
former District Attorney
Height: 1.83 m
Weight: 82.5 kg
Base: Gotham City
Allies: The Secret Society,
Gilda Dent
Foes: Batman, the Batman
Family, Erin McKillen

POWERS AND ABILITIES

Cunning strategist; expert
knowledge of law and
police procedure; split
personality causes
extreme unpredictability.

TWO SIDES OF THE SAME COIN

Harvey Dent and his
old friend Bruce Wayne
have become enemies
as Two-Face and
Batman. With a flip
of his special coin,
Two-Face lets luck
dictate his every
decision — good or evil.

Gotham City's District Attorney,
Harvey Dent, led a promising life as the
city's golden boy. But when he crossed
Erin McKillen of the organised crime
family known as the McKillen Clan,
his life changed forever. Erin took
revenge upon Harvey and his family.
The trauma of this tragic event
released Harvey's dark side, and he took
on the persona of the criminal Two-Face.

*"Chance **trumps** choice **every
second of every day.**"*

Handsome
features are now
forever marred

Scarred two-
headed coin to
match his face

Wears
two-toned
clothing

THE JOKER'S DAUGHTER

ROGUE

VITAL STATS

Real Name: Duela Dent

Occupation: Criminal, leader of underground cult

Height: 1.63 m

Weight: 54 kg

Base: Gotham City

Allies: Suicide Squad

Foes: Catwoman, Batman, Batgirl

POWERS AND ABILITIES

Criminal mastermind; uses the Joker's urban legend to her advantage; manic fighter; employs moon-shaped blade for combat.

CLOWN PRINCESS
The Joker's Daughter gained followers when she took control of an underground tribe in the Nethers. Obsessed with the Joker, she has run afoul of Batman, Catwoman and Batgirl in her short criminal career.

Duela was a disturbed young woman living with her family in the Gotham City suburbs. After her face was scarred during a botched surgery, she fled for the grime and squalour of Gotham City's underground tunnels. There she discovered the Joker's lost skin mask. In a grab for power, she adopted it as her own face, becoming the so-called Joker's Daughter.

Clad in the Joker's colours: purple and green

Wears the Joker's skin as a mask

Staff often has moon-shaped blade

Shirt design implies the Joker is her father

"Hit me like one of your super-villains, Batman!"

BANE

VITAL STATS

Real Name: Unknown
Occupation: Criminal
Height: 2.03 m
Weight: 159 kg (193 kg on Venom)
Base: Gotham City
Allies: Santa Prisca mercenaries
Foes: Batman, the Batman Family, Batwoman

POWERS AND ABILITIES

Extremely intelligent with an iron-clad will; brilliant strategist; skilled hand-to-hand fighter; enhanced strength, durability, weight and endurance due to use of super-steroid Venom.

BREAKING BAT

Bane lives with one goal in mind: to break the Batman. Bane had heard legends of the Dark Knight while in his native country of Santa Prisca, and yearned to conquer the seemingly untamable Gotham City and its dark protector.

Born in the corrupt nation of Santa Prisca, the boy who would become Bane grew up in its cruellest prison, Pena Duro, becoming a hardened yet well-read man. The prison doctors injected him with a powerful steroid called Venom. Not only did the steroid work, it gave Bane the strength he needed to escape and set his sights on Gotham City.

Always equipped with Venom supply

Venom injected directly into head

Huge exterior can overshadow brilliant mind

Often leads army of Santa Prisca soldiers

"Only when I'm dead do I intend to rest."

CLAYFACE

VITAL STATS

Real Name: Basil Karlo

Occupation: Criminal, former actor

Height: Varies

Weight: Varies

Base: Gotham City

Allies: Poison Ivy, the Unknowns, Batwoman

Foes: Batman, the Batman Family

POWERS AND ABILITIES

Made of living clay that can bend and shape to his will; able to impersonate others by taking their exact shape and DNA; highly skilled actor.

IMPRESSIONABLE

While Clayface has primarily been an enemy of Batman, he briefly joined forces with Batwoman and a team called the Unknowns when he suffered from amnesia. He has since reverted to his criminal ways.

When Clayface takes on the forms of others, he now adopts their DNA. He can be anyone by just touching them; anyone but the man he once was.

Basil Karlo was a famous actor, known primarily for his roles in horror films. However, when replaced as the lead in a movie, he turned to murder. His life began to take a strange path when he injected himself with a formula that altered his body completely, making him a shape-changer made of living clay. He became Clayface, one of Batman's most powerful enemies.

"...I ain't your daddy's Clayface!"

RĀ'S AL GHŪL

VITAL STATS

Real Name: Unknown
Occupation: International terrorist
Height: 1.96 m
Weight: 97.5 kg
Base: 'Eth Alth'eban
Allies: The League of Assassins, Talia al Ghūl
Foes: Batman, Robin, the Batman Family

POWERS AND ABILITIES

Extremely long-life through his unprecedented access to the anti-ageing Lazarus Pits; expert swordsman; highly skilled martial artist and fighter; genius intellect; master strategist.

HEIR APPARENT

Despite living for hundreds of years due to the Lazarus Pits, Rā's al Ghūl knows that he will die one day. He has tried hard to make Batman take on the role as his successor, but the Dark Knight constantly rejects his offer.

Legend tells of Rā's al Ghūl walking the Earth for the last 700 years. He adopted the name "The Demon's Head" after the death of his wife. Prolonging his own life through restorative Lazarus Pits, Rā's has amassed an entire League of Assassins with the goal of destroying the majority of the population in order to shape the world in his cruel image.

"My League of Assassins will tear this world apart..."

Speaks many different languages

Ageing slowed thanks to Lazarus Pits

Ornate gold detailing

Wears regal clothing fit for a ruler

TALIA AL GHŪL

VITAL STATS

Full Name: Talia al Ghūl
Occupation: International terrorist
Height: 1.73 m
Weight: 54 kg
Base: Mobile
Allies: Rā's al Ghūl, Leviathan, Red Hood, the League of Assassins
Foes: Batman, Robin, the Batman Family, Batman, Inc.

POWERS AND ABILITIES

Access to huge terrorist networks; superb fighter and assassin; extremely intelligent with a mind for strategy; charismatic leader; worked her way into both Batman and Robin's hearts.

IN THE NAME OF THE FATHER

While she stayed by his side for years, Talia al Ghūl later parted ways with her father. She formed her own terrorist organisation called Leviathan, and set out to destroy Batman once and for all.

Uses laboratories for immoral experiments

Beauty causes some to drop their guard

Wears expensive regal attire

Talia al Ghūl is the daughter of the terrorist Rā's al Ghūl, and grew up learning the evil methods of being an assassin. When she met Batman, the two were instantly attracted to one another and had a short-lived romance that resulted in the birth of their son, Damian Wayne. While leading the criminal organisation Leviathan, Talia was shot and presumably killed.

"Look into the eye of the gorgon."

THE LEAGUE OF ASSASSINS

VITAL STATS

Team Name: The League of Assassins

Base: 'Eth Alth'eban

Allies: Rā's al Ghūl, Talia al Ghūl, Red Hood

Foes: Batman, the Batman Family, Deathstroke, the Untitled

Notable Members: Rā's al Ghūl, Talia al Ghūl, Lady Shiva, Bronze Tiger, Cheshire, December Graystone, Rictus, Dr. Darrk, Red Hood (former), Anya Volkova (former)

EVE OF DESTRUCTION

Always pursuing immortality, Rā's al Ghūl sent the League of Assassins to Mother Eve, hoping to learn the secret of her de-ageing process. Fortunately, Batgirl and the Birds of Prey were on hand to defend their ally.

Formed by the international terrorist Rā's al Ghūl, the League of Assassins is an elite and clandestine organisation based in the mystical city of 'Eth Alth'eban. The League is usually led by Rā's, whose ultimate goal is to destroy a significant portion of the world's population in order to shape what is left into a world of his choosing.

"We are the League of Assassins. We are death incarnate."

Rā's al Ghūl takes a hands-on approach as leader of the League of Assassins. He is very often present during its missions.

LADY SHIVA

VITAL STATS

Real Name: Sandra Wu-San

Occupation: Mercenary

Height: 1.73 m

Weight: 52 kg

Base: 'Eth Alth'eban

Allies: The League of Assassins, Rā's al Ghūl, Ninja Man-Bats

Foes: Batman, Dick Grayson, the Untitled

POWERS AND ABILITIES

Arguably the world's greatest martial artist; master of many weapons; commands army of Ninja Man-Bats when working with the League of Assassins; brilliant and cunning mind.

SHIVA THE DESTROYER

When Dick Grayson was Robin, he interrupted a fight between Batman and Lady Shiva. Lady Shiva has the skill to read fighting styles like language, so when she later met Grayson in his Nightwing guise, she instantly recognised him.

Thinks several steps ahead of her opponents

Expert at nearly every type of traditional weapon

Even her hair is weaponised with a blade

Lady Shiva is considered one of the world's greatest assassins, and boasts a long history with Batman and his allies. As a member of the League of Assassins, Shiva has worked directly for Rā's al Ghūl, as well as commanded her own missions. Despite working with the League, Lady Shiva is most often found alone, committing one assassination after another.

"Fear us. Fear me. Lady Shiva!"

MR FREEZE

VITAL STATS

Real Name: Dr Victor Fries

Occupation: Criminal, former scientist

Height: 1.83 m

Weight: 86 kg

Base: Gotham City

Allies: Starling, Scarecrow, Harley Quinn, Merrymaker, Professor Pyg

Foes: Batman, the Batman Family, the Birds of Prey, the Court of Owls

POWERS AND ABILITIES

Refrigerated suit gives him superhuman strength and endurance; developed quick-freeze technology in the form of freeze guns and grenades; genius-level intellect.

ICE IN HIS VEINS

With a body temperature of 23 degrees Fahrenheit, Victor Fries was fitted with special goggles to keep his eyes from freezing. He developed a refrigerated exoskeleton and an arsenal of cold weapons to become Mr Freeze.

Mr Freeze is obsessed with Nora Fields and believes they were married before she was frozen. He'll kill anyone that hampers finding her a cure.

When Victor Fries was just a boy, his mother died in a frozen lake. As an adult, he took a job at Wayne Enterprises' cryogenics lab, where he focused on freezing bodies. He became obsessed with the frozen body of a woman he'd never met, Nora Fields. When Bruce Wayne closed his division, Fries lashed out, causing a lab accident that transformed him into Mr Freeze.

"You don't understand what you're meddling with, Batman."

KILLER CROC

VITAL STATS

Real Name: Waylon Jones
Occupation: Criminal
Height: 1.96 m
Weight: 121.5 kg
Base: Gotham City
Allies: Arsenal, Catwoman
Foes: Batman, the Batman Family, Bane

POWERS AND ABILITIES

Enhanced strength, durability and endurance due to rare skin condition; excellent fighter with a history of wrestling alligators.

LURKING IN THE SEWERS

On the surface, Killer Croc can be perceived as simple muscle, but in the sewers he commands respect. Croc knows the underground inside and out, and has even ruled over tribes of vagabonds. He is known to them as King Croc.

Waylon Jones was raised by his Aunt Flowers in the poor neighbourhood of Crown Point in Gotham City. Born with a skin condition that caused scale growth all over his body, Waylon knew no other life aside from one in a circus sideshow. Frustrated with his low pay and, after biting his employer while in a rage, Jones ventured into a life of crime as Killer Croc.

"Death by Croc."

Teeth filed to sharp points

Extremely strong and muscular

Skin tough and difficult to pierce

CARMINE FALCONE

VITAL STATS

Full Name: Carmine Falcone

Occupation: Crime boss

Height: 1.85 m

Weight: 93 kg

Base: Gotham City

Allies: Mayor Sebastian Hady, Jack Forbes, Tiger Shark

Foes: Batman, Catwoman, James Gordon, the Penguin

POWERS AND ABILITIES

Powerful crime boss; highly connected in Gotham City's underworld; amassed wealth through illegal means; intelligent, strategic mind; years of criminal experience.

ET TU, CATWOMAN?

During Batman's campaign to drive Falcone out of Gotham City, Catwoman lashed out at the crime boss, scarring his face with her claws. Falcone has sought revenge against Catwoman ever since.

It took the combined efforts of Batman and James Gordon to run the organised crime boss Carmine "the Roman" Falcone out of Gotham City. So when Falcone returned to the city when Gordon was wrongly imprisoned, it was certainly cause for concern. Carmine's second stay in Gotham City was cut short, however, when he was arrested by the G.C.P.D.'s Jason Bard.

"This city won't let me lose."

Carmine Falcone is good at making enemies. He was once abducted by Professor Pyg and his animal-masked gang before Batman saved his life.

REX "THE LION" CALABRESE

VITAL STATS

Full Name: Rex Calabrese

Occupation: Former crime boss

Height: 1.83 m

Weight: 120 kg

Base: Gotham City

Allies: Catwoman, the Calabrese Crime family

Foes: Carmine Falcone, Batman, the Penguin

POWERS AND ABILITIES

Powerful former crime boss; highly connected in Gotham City's underworld; amassed wealth through illegal means; intelligent, strategic mind; years of criminal experience.

LUCK OF THE LION

Named "Leo" by fellow inmates, Calabrese has spent the last several years in Blackgate Penitentiary. His former protégé, Carmine Falcone, thought he had killed Calabrese, and had no idea he was hiding in jail.

Rex "The Lion" Calabrese was once one of the most powerful underworld figures in Gotham City. His career was thought to be cut short when he was "killed" by a former ally. In reality, Rex was in hiding, and eventually made contact with his daughter, Selina Kyle, to persuade her to take over the family crime business. She agreed, although she harboured many angry feelings towards him.

"The cat's outta the bag, so to speak."

When Catwoman's father first approached her to unite Gotham City's crime families, she lashed out, angry that he had abandoned her.

ANTHONY ZUCCO

VITAL STATS

Full Name: Anthony Zucco

Occupation: Criminal, former mayor's aide

Height: 1.83 m

Weight: 109 kg

Base: Chicago

Ally: Mayor Wallace Cole

Foes: Dick Grayson, Sophia Branch, Prankster, Batman

POWERS AND ABILITIES

Intelligent strategist; many criminal connections in the Gotham City underworld and in Chicago; personal friend of the mayor of Chicago; uses firearm.

ACCEPTING RESPONSIBILITY

Tony Zucco attempted to turn his life around in Chicago, assuming the fake name Billy Lester, marrying and having a child. When Nightwing tracked him down, Zucco finally came clean and admitted his guilt.

Tony Zucco was a shakedown artist with plans to make a name for himself. When attempting to gain protection money from Haly's Circus, Zucco threatened C.C. Haly, a crime a young Dick Grayson witnessed. So when Dick's parents were murdered during their trapeze routine, he knew who the culprit was. Dick hunted Zucco, but the criminal faked his own death.

"...what I did to the Graysons... there's no excuse I can make."

Tony Zucco did much harm in Gotham City. His daughter, however, distanced herself from him by changing her name to Sonia Branch.

JOE CHILL

VITAL STATS

Full Name: Joe Chill
Occupation: Criminal
Height: 1.73 m
Weight: 81.5 kg
Base: Gotham City
Allies: Unknown
Foes: Batman, Thomas and Martha Wayne

POWERS AND ABILITIES

Common street criminal with access to a handgun.

CHILL OF THE NIGHT

Joe Chill happened upon the Waynes when they were exiting a movie on Gotham City's Park Row. He was startled by Martha Wayne's scream, and shot her and her husband.

When young Bruce Wayne's parents were gunned down before his eyes, his life was forever changed. Although he suspected the Court of Owls or some other nefarious organisation of being the culprit, he later learnt that the killer was Joe Chill, after a witness identified the murderer. Bruce tracked Chill to his apartment, to discover not a mastermind, but a petty criminal.

"I didn't mean to."

When Bruce Wayne finally tracked down Chill, he planned to kill him. However, Bruce couldn't pull the trigger, and instead let the sad man live.

THE COURT OF OWLS

VITAL STATS

Team Name: The Court of Owls

Base: Gotham City

Allies: Army of Talons and fellow secret Owl members

Foes: Batman, Bane, Talon (Calvin Rose), Lincoln March

Notable Past Members: Benjamin Orchard, John Wycliffe, Maria Powers, Joseph Powers, Sebastian Clark, Lincoln March

GRIPPED BY TALONS

Batman mistakenly suspected the Court of Owls was behind his parents' murder. He first encountered the Court when he was trapped in their labyrinth beneath Gotham City, and he barely managed to escape.

A cult as old as Gotham City itself, the Court of Owls is a secret society of the most nefarious order. Clandestinely controlling politics and the evolution of the city from behind closed doors, the Court employs an elite army of Talons — loyal assassins who murder their enemies from the shadows. Batman stopped a troubling resurgence, but the Court is still alive in Gotham City.

"...Beware the Court of Owls, that watches all the time..."

Members wear owl masks to hide identities

Children brainwashed at young age

Order members are typically society's richest

TALON

ROGUE

VITAL STATS

Real Name: William Cobb
Occupation: Assassin for the Court of Owls
Height: 1.91 m
Weight: 100 kg
Base: Gotham City
Allies: The Court of Owls
Foes: Batman, Dick Grayson, the Batman Family

POWERS AND ABILITIES

Expertly trained assassin; natural fighter and trained martial artist; superb at knife throwing; has healing ability and can be resurrected from the dead; long-lived and experienced.

CAPE VS CLAW

When Bruce Wayne was targeted by Talon, Batman began investigating the Court of Owls. This led him to discover the Court's labyrinth, where he was forced to combat Cobb and just barely triumphed over him to escape.

William Cobb, one of the Court of Owls's finest Talon assassins, is the great-grandfather of Dick Grayson. Growing up poor on the streets of Gotham City in the early 1900s, Cobb was recruited into Haly's Circus where he became an expert knife handler. Cobb soon became a Talon for the Court of Owls, later offering his "gray son" to Haly's Circus for training.

> *"Bruce Wayne. The Court of Owls has sentenced you to die."*

Uses owls and owl imagery to threaten

Wears owl-like enhanced goggles

Expert knife thrower

Each Talon wears a different uniform

LINCOLN MARCH

VITAL STATS

Real Name: Unknown
Occupation: Criminal
Height: 1.93 m
Weight: 104 kg
Base: Gotham City
Ally: Cluemaster
Foes: Batman, the Court of Owls, the Batman Family

POWERS AND ABILITIES

Skilled combatant; advanced armoured Talon suit allows for flight, enhanced strength and durability; suit is fitted with hi-tech devices; brilliant strategist with powerful underworld connections; healing abilities; can be resurrected from the dead.

MARCH ON GOTHAM CITY

After dying and then being regenerated by the Court of Owls, Lincoln March adopted an owl costume and battled Batman. March wanted to destroy the Dark Knight, but he also killed fellow Owls in order to steal their riches.

Despite his claims to the contrary, the true origin of Lincoln March remains a mystery. He insists he is Thomas Wayne, Jr, Bruce Wayne's younger brother who was believed to have died in a car crash. According to March, he was placed in Willowwood Home for Children by his parents after Martha Wayne's car accident, and was forgotten after their death.

Is taller than his "brother" Batman

Has taken Owls's healing serum to be resurrected

Often trades civilian clothes for Talon suit

"Brother to brother...
owl to bat!"

THE DEALER

VITAL STATS

Real Name: Etienne Guiborg
Occupation: Auctioneer
of illegal goods
Height: 1.68 m
Weight: 54 kg
Base: Gotham City
Ally: Mirror House
Foes: Dick Grayson,
Batman

POWERS AND ABILITIES
Connections to a large
criminal network able to
secure various illegal and
contraband items for him;
extremely intelligent and
manipulative; uses Venom
and an outdated Man-Bat
formula to turn into a large
and super-strong bat-like
creature.

A REAL GAS AT PARTIES
To ensure his auctions are
exclusive and anonymous,
the Dealer fills the room
with a poisonous gas and
requires all the participants
to hide their identities
behind life-saving gas masks.

Dick Grayson first became aware of
the Dealer when he briefly took over
the role of Batman in Bruce Wayne's
absence. Discovering evidence missing
from the G.C.P.D., Batman followed a
trail to locate a secret society called
"Mirror House". Entering one of their
auctions under a fake name, Grayson
was discovered and nearly killed by
the Dealer's people before escaping.

> "There you have it — the
> market has spoken!"

The Dealer ran into Nightwing when he
attempted to sell a circus costume worn by John
Grayson that had been vandalised by the Joker.

MAN-BAT

VITAL STATS

Real Name: Dr Kirk Langstrom

Occupation: Scientist and science teacher, acting head of S.H.A.D.E. Security

Height: 1.85 m

Weight: 91 kg

Base: Gotham City

Allies: Gotham Academy, S.H.A.D.E., the Outlaws

Foes: Batman, Bat-Queen, the Batman Family

POWERS AND ABILITIES

Serum transforms him into a monstrous Man-Bat with enhanced strength, speed, agility and endurance, with capability of flight; genius-level intellect.

BAT VS MAN

While Kirk's savagery as Man-Bat has put him at odds with Batman, he has recently found a way to control his transformations, now taking jobs at the clandestine operation S.H.A.D.E., as well as at Gotham Academy.

Dr Kirk Langstrom is a noble scientist who wanted to find a cure for the deaf. He developed the Langstrom Atavistic Gene Recall Serum, but unfortunately it transformed its victims into hideous humanoid bat creatures. When a sample of the serum was stolen and unleashed on Gotham City, Kirk injected himself with an anti-virus. This cured the innocents but left Kirk as the sole remaining Man-Bat.

> *"I had **to become** the creature."*

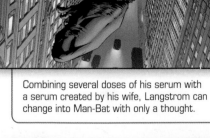

Combining several doses of his serum with a serum created by his wife, Langstrom can change into Man-Bat with only a thought.

BAT-QUEEN

VITAL STATS

Real Name: Francine Langstrom (Felicity Lee)
Occupation: Criminal and corporate spy
Height: 1.80 m
Weight: 76.5 kg
Base: Gotham City
Ally: Wrath
Foes: Man-Bat, Batman, G.C.P.D.

POWERS AND ABILITIES

Serum transforms her into a monstrous She-Bat with enhanced strength, speed, agility and endurance, with capability of flight; controls army of piranha-like bats; manipulative and ruthless.

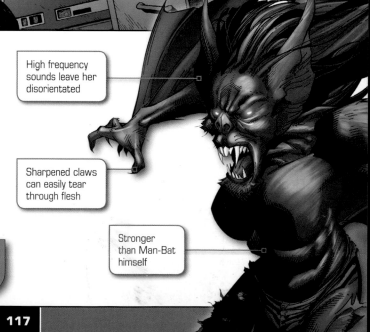

QUEEN OF THE NIGHT

As the villain Bat-Queen, Francine Langstrom's main opposition was her husband, Kirk. Angered that his wife had married him under false pretenses, Kirk wanted nothing more than to put an end to his wife's wicked ways.

The wife of Dr Kirk Langstrom, who would become Man-Bat, Francine Langstrom's real name is Felicity Lee. A spy tasked with keeping an eye on Kirk's scientific work for her boss, E.D. Caldwell, Francine wanted to help her employer create a biological weapon from Kirk's findings. Creating her own imperfect Man-Bat formula, Francine became the highly unstable Bat-Queen.

"...I am – the Bat-Queen! Screeeee!"

High frequency sounds leave her disorientated

Sharpened claws can easily tear through flesh

Stronger than Man-Bat himself

BRONZE TIGER

VITAL STATS

Real Name: Ben Turner
Occupation: Mercenary
Height: 1.80 m
Weight: 89 kg
Base: 'Eth Alth'eban
Allies: Rā's al Ghūl, the League of Assassins, Deathstroke
Foes: The Untitled, Batman

POWERS AND ABILITIES

One of the world's best martial artists; proficient in a variety of fighting styles and weapons; contacts in the espionage and criminal worlds; access to the League of Assassins's assets; able to shift into animalistic tiger form; often wears tiger-themed armour into battle.

TIGER STYLE

An old drinking buddy of Deathstroke's, the Bronze Tiger nevertheless agreed to kill his friend when his mind was being manipulated. Despite working directly with fellow assassin Lady Shiva on this mission, the Tiger was unsuccessful.

Ben Turner is a ranking member of the clandestine mercenary group, the League of Assassins. His ability to transform into a tiger is a useful asset, although it comes at a price. When the vigilante Red Hood was recruited to briefly lead the group, the Bronze Tiger welcomed him. While it is known that he is Deathstroke's old friend, his past remains a mystery.

"Do yourself a favour and yield."

The Bronze Tiger has a talisman that "burns away" at his soul every time he transforms into a tiger. Nonetheless, he often finds it useful in a fight.

DR DARRK

VITAL STATS

Real Name: Dr Ebenezer Darcel

Occupation: Criminal

Height: 2.24 m

Weight: 175 kg

Base: Mobile

Allies: The League of Assassins, Rā's al Ghūl

Foes: Batman, Talon, Lord Death Man

POWERS AND ABILITIES

Forced to live in a cybernetic body that allows him superhuman strength, endurance and durability; highly intelligent; access to the assets of the League of Assassins.

LORDING OVER DEATH

As Rā's al Ghūl's employee, the now cybernetically-enhanced Dr Darrk attempted to mine the secret of Lord Death Man's immortality by extracting the so-called Shelley Formula from his very blood.

When Batman first met Talia al Ghūl, the two became allies when he rescued her from the clutches of Dr Darrk. While Batman had no idea that Talia's father, Rā's al Ghūl, was the head of the notorious League of Assassins, and that Dr Darrk had fallen out with his employer, Batman took Talia's side, and comforted her when it appeared she had shot and killed Dr Darrk.

Dr Darrk did not die at Talia's hands. Resurfacing as a member of the League of Assassins, he later attempted to best Batman using hallucinogenic gas.

"I've prepared a welcome for our would-be nemesis, our dark pursuer."

DOLLMAKER

VITAL STATS

Real Name: Barton Mathis
Occupation: Criminal
Height: 1.85 m
Weight: 76.5 kg
Base: Gotham City
Allies: The Joker, the Joker's Daughter, Dollhouse
Foes: Batman, the Batman Family, James Gordon

POWERS AND ABILITIES

Skilled surgeon capable of stitching living and dead bodies together to form gruesome "dolls"; intelligent yet twisted mind.

FAMILY MAN

The Dollmaker has passed on his gruesome pastime to his family members, including his son Bentley and his associates Jack-in-the-Box and Sampson. He also has a daughter called Dollhouse, who once battled Catwoman.

The son of serial killer Wesley Mathis, Barton Mathis watched his father get shot down by James Gordon. Seeking revenge, and now calling himself the Dollmaker, he kidnapped the police commissioner, only to have Batman interrupt his scheme. Dollmaker created his most infamous work of "art" when he cut skin from the Joker's face.

Wears mask made from victims' skin

Gifted surgeon with great medical expertise

"This will only hurt—a lot."

MR MOSAIC

VITAL STATS

Real Name: Unknown
Occupation: Criminal
Height: 1.70 m
Weight: 94 kg
Base: Gotham City
Allies: Emperor Blackgate,
Mr Combustible,
Imperceptible Man,
Mr Toxic
Foes: Batman, the
Batman Family, G.C.P.D.

POWERS AND ABILITIES

Has extensive ties in the
political and criminal world;
wealthy, and hires others
to do his dirty work for him.

THE LONG GAME
Mr Mosaic talks a big game, but
when confronted with physical
danger, he backs down from his
larger-than-life persona quite
quickly. Instead, he bides his
time and looks for an opportunity
for revenge down the line.

Little is known about how Mr Mosaic
rose to power in Gotham City's
underworld, or even how he developed
his bizarre skin condition. What is
known, however, is that he is very
influential in the criminal scene, and
has worked with Emperor Blackgate.
He raided the docks for the gang leader
while the rest of Gotham City was busy
dealing with Blackgate's Man-Bat virus.

*"Think a hitchhiker with a face
like this can get a ride?"*

Mr Mosaic was one of the criminals freed
by Bane when the villain organised a massive
breakout at Blackgate Penitentiary.

HUGO STRANGE

VITAL STATS

Full Name: Dr Hugo Strange
Occupation: Psychiatrist,
school counsellor, criminal
Height: 1.79 m
Weight: 77 kg
Base: Gotham City
Allies: Eli Strange,
Crazy Quilt, Dr Death
Foes: Batman, the
Batman Family

POWERS AND ABILITIES

Extremely persuasive
and manipulative; expert
scientist known for his
unorthodox experiments;
well connected in the
criminal underground
and Super Hero community;
highly intelligent; in excellent
physical condition.

THE DOCTOR IS IN

A bit of a psychiatrist
to the stars when not
plotting the downfall of
Batman, Hugo Strange
has been known to give
personal counsel to
Arsenal, Red Hood's
partner and longtime
Outlaws teammate.

It has been difficult for Batman to
prove the corrupt nature of Professor
Hugo Strange. Despite their frequent
clashes, Hugo keeps reemerging in
the Dark Knight's life in various
legitimate positions. One of the
infamous Doctors Three alongside
Crazy Quilt and Dr Death, Hugo is
now a counsellor at Gotham Academy,
as if his past crimes never occurred.

*"I'll keep our talks a secret.
I am here to help you."*

Strange takes pride in manipulating the minds
of others for his own selfish gain, especially the
aspiring young students at Gotham Academy.

MR ZSASZ

VITAL STATS

Full Name: Victor Zsasz
Occupation: Criminal
Height: 1.73 m
Weight: 68 kg
Base: Gotham City
Ally: Emperor Blackgate
Foes: Batman, the Penguin, Merrymaker

POWERS AND ABILITIES

Deadly efficient murderer; excellent physical condition; mentally unstable and obsessed with murder; usually prefers using blades or knives.

DEATH TALLY

One of Gotham City's most dangerous and psychotic villains, Mr Zsasz likes to keep a tally of his kills. For every person he murders, he carves a notch in his own flesh to remember them by.

Victor Zsasz has an addictive personality, and was therefore an easy mark when he gambled in the Penguin's Iceberg Casino. The heir to Zsasz Industries, Victor lost all his money thanks to the Penguin encouraging his love of gambling. Victor's mind snapped, and he embarked on a killing spree that continues to this day, despite Batman's efforts to stop him.

"The bird-man. This was all his doing. He gave me the knife."

While he usually prefers to work alone, Zsasz has been the willing pawn of Emperor Blackgate in the past, helping to spread the Man-Bat virus.

THE CRIME SYNDICATE

VITAL STATS

Group Name: The Crime Syndicate

Base: Happy Harbour, Rhode Island

Allies: The Secret Society

Foes: The Justice League, Mazahs, Lex Luthor, the Justice League of America

Members:
Owlman, Ultraman, Superwoman, Power Ring (deceased), Johnny Quick (deceased), Atomica (deceased), Sea King (deceased), Deathstorm (deceased), Grid (deceased)

INJUSTICE FOR ALL

The Crime Syndicate are the evil equivalent of the Justice League, headed by three notorious super-villains: Ultraman is the dark mirror to Superman, Superwoman is the corrupted version of Wonder Woman and Owlman is Earth-Three's evil Batman.

In the parallel dimension of Earth-Three, evil overshadows good. There, the Crime Syndicate served as an evil Justice League of sorts. When the Crime Syndicate fled to the Justice League's dimension, they banished the Justice League to a prison inside the matrix of the hero Firestorm. Meanwhile, they caused a planet-wide blackout and declared themselves rulers of the world.

"This world is ours."

Despite uniting the world's super-villains, the Crime Syndicate finally fell when Batman and a team of villains invaded the Syndicate's headquarters.

SIGNALMAN

VITAL STATS

Real Name: Phil Cobb
Occupation: Criminal
Height: 1.88 m
Weight: 91 kg
Base: Gotham City
Allies: Blockbuster, the Secret Society, Firefly, Cluemaster, Lock-Up
Foes: Batman, the Batman Family

POWERS AND ABILITIES

Employs a variety of signal-themed gadgets; very intelligent, with strong computer hacking skills; keeps himself in excellent physical condition; cultivates connections with many minor criminals.

ANSWERING THE SIGNAL

The Signalman seems to join any club that will have him as a member, so it made complete sense when he was an early supporter of the villain Outsider and a member of the nefarious Secret Society.

Small-time criminal Phil Cobb decided to up his game when he reached Gotham City after seeing the Bat-Signal shining over the skyline. He opted for the identity of Signalman, and his sign-themed robberies soon drew Batman's attention. Involved in Cluemaster and Lincoln March's plan to kill the Dark Knight, he also played a major role in the Secret Society.

"In this town, you learn not to assume anything."

One of Signalman's greatest strengths is his ability to hack into a city's traffic system, controlling the traffic lights as he sees fit.

BLOCKBUSTER

VITAL STATS

Real Name: Mark Desmond
Occupation: Criminal
Height: 2.44 m
Weight: 374 kg
Base: Gotham City
Allies: The Secret Society, the Fist of Cain, Roland Desmond
Foes: Batman, Hawkman, the Batman Family, Superman

POWERS AND ABILITIES

Superhuman strength, durability and endurance; almost completely incapable of thought; prone to fits of rage.

BATTLE OF THE BLOCKBUSTERS

When Blockbuster returned to his enormous form, he fought another transformed patient, Professor Ziegler. However, after defeat at Blockbuster's hands, Ziegler returned to his normal human state.

Chemist Mark Desmond was working on a treatment that would stop violent behaviour. However, he was accidentally transformed into a raging behemoth called Blockbuster. After battles with Batman, Robin and Superman, he found himself at the Rest Haven medical facility — human again and being treated for dementia. But soon, steroid treatments restored his monstrous Blockbuster form.

> *"I am Blockbuster — and I crush all!"*

Blockbuster later joined the infamous Secret Society where his brute strength is a powerful weapon in the clandestine group's arsenal.

COPPERHEAD

VITAL STATS

Real Name: Unknown

Occupation: Criminal

Height: 1.88 m

Weight: 86 kg

Base: Mobile

Allies: The Secret Society, Knightfall

Foes: The Birds of Prey, Batman, Catwoman, Deathstroke

POWERS AND ABILITIES

Expert contortionist able to move through small spaces; snake-like ability to squeeze opponents; enhanced agility, durability and endurance; possesses sharp fangs.

TWO AGAINST ONE

Copperhead once took on Black Canary above the streets of Baltimore. As they battled near an electronic billboard, the Justice League made the billboard flash a bright white light to momentarily blind the snake and help Black Canary win.

An old foe of Batman's, the serpentine villain Copperhead joined the Secret Society after learning that they had a way to get villains out of trouble. Unlike other Secret Society members, however, he wanted nothing more than to attack Batman head on. This attitude led to his downfall when he and several other Secret Society members made their attack.

"It's easier if you don't fight."

Taking on the Justice League proved unwise. Copperhead lost a fight with Black Canary, and was then killed by Deathstroke.

THE MAD HATTER

VITAL STATS

Real Name: Jervis Tetch

Occupation: Criminal

Height: 1.42 m

Weight: 67.5 kg

Base: Gotham City

Allies: Tweedledee, Tweedledum

Foes: Batman, Red Robin, Bluebird, Black Mask, Anarky

POWERS AND ABILITIES

Extremely intelligent; brilliant inventor and technician; uses drugged teas to enhance his own physical abilities; fanatically obsessed with Lewis Carroll's stories and poems; creations let him control the minds of others.

BATTLE OF THE MINDS

The Mad Hatter drinks a variety of drugged teas to give himself an advantage in a fight. Depending on the mixture, his teas can give him heightened pain tolerance or superhuman strength.

Obsessed with hats and Lewis Carroll's classic *Alice in Wonderland* stories, a young Jervis Tetch fell in love with his classmate, Alice. When she spurned him, he used testosterone enhancers to help his body grow, but instead developed violent tendencies. Years later, as the Mad Hatter, he uses his gift for invention to ensure that no one will ever reject him again.

Hat contains mind control technology

Often quotes Carroll during encounters

Attire based on Lewis Carroll's Mad Hatter

"No one gets between me and my beloved!"

HUSH

VITAL STATS

Real Name: Dr Thomas Elliot

Occupation: Criminal, surgeon

Height: 1.91 m

Weight: 100 kg

Base: Gotham City

Allies: Jason Bard, Architect, the Riddler

Foes: Batman, Julia and Alfred Pennyworth

POWERS AND ABILITIES

Gifted surgeon; brilliant strategist; strong connections to criminal underworld; knows Batman's secret identity; athletic; trained in hand-to-hand combat; highly efficient with firearms.

FRIENDLY FIRE

Hush has always envied Bruce Wayne, and wanted to be exactly like him. After learning that Bruce Wayne is really Batman, Hush's resolve to destroy Wayne's life became even stronger, often lashing out at those close to him.

Tommy Elliot was Bruce Wayne's childhood best friend. After Bruce's parents died, the disturbed Tommy wanted to be an orphan too. As a teenager, Tommy began to imitate Bruce Wayne even more, causing a falling out between the former friends. No longer under Bruce's good influence, Tommy began on a downward spiral, becoming the villain Hush.

Wrapped face in bandages after scarring himself

Utility Belt similar to the Dark Knight's

Can operate firearm with either hand

"I'm just like you, Bruce. I'm just like you."

THE SECRET SOCIETY

VITAL STATS

Group Name: The Secret Society
Base: Mobile
Allies: The Crime Syndicate
Foes: The Justice League,
The Justice League of America

Notable Members:
Outsider (deceased),
Scarecrow, Professor Ivo,
Copperhead (deceased),
Amazo, Dr Psycho,
Multiplex, Blockbuster,
Signalman, Shaggy Man

SOCIETY OF SIN
To form his Secret Society, the Outsider gathered
together some of the most nefarious faces from
Batman's Rogues Gallery like Copperhead,
Signalman and Blockbuster, as well as enemies of
the Justice League, like the android Amazo.

The evil Crime Syndicate of Earth-
Three wanted to destroy its heroic
counterpart, the Justice League.
Syndicate member Owlman sent his
butler, the Outsider, into the Justice
League's world on a covert mission.
The Outsider gathered the Justice
League's enemies into a Secret
Society of super-villains, paving the
way for the arrival of the Syndicate.

> *"...as you say on your world...*
> *the butler did it."*

The Outsider is a villainous Earth-Three version of
Alfred. He uses a mystical device called Pandora's
Box to create a gateway into another dimension.

DARKSEID

VITAL STATS

Real Name: Uxas

Occupation: Ruler of
Apokolips

Height: 2.67 m

Weight: 023 kg

Base: Apokolips

Allies: Desaad, Kalibak,
Granny Goodness,
Parademons

Foes: The Justice League,
Batman, Superman,
Highfather, Orion

POWERS AND ABILITIES

Omega Effect eye beams can
kill, resurrect, harm or send
victims hurtling through time;
superhuman strength and
endurance; commands armies
of Parademons, elite soldiers
and a planet of minions.

GOD AMONG MEN

Darkseid had conquered
many worlds before,
including Earth-Two,
a parallel dimension to
the Earth of the Justice
League. So when the
League chased him off their
planet, he swore revenge.

The planet Apokolips has been at
war with its neighbouring world New
Genesis for years. Darkseid is the ruler
of Apokolips and wants nothing less
than to achieve mastery over death and
rule the universe. To that end, he has
clashed with the Justice League and
Batman, when the Dark Knight travelled
to Apokolips to rescue the body of
the temporarily dead Damian Wayne.

Eyes produce
devastating
Omega Beams

Stone-like body
can overpower
even Superman

Towers over
members of the
Justice League

"You came a long way to die."

SUICIDE SQUAD

VITAL STATS

Team Name: Task Force X, Suicide Squad

Base: Belle Reve Penitentiary

Allies: Amanda Waller, Vic Sage, James Gordon, Jr

Foes: Deathstroke, Basilisk, The League

Members: Deadshot, Harley Quinn, Captain Boomerang, Reverse-Flash, Parasite, Black Manta, King Shark (former), the Joker's Daughter (former), Cheetah (former), Savant (former), Unknown Soldier (former), Iceberg (former), Crowbar (former), El Diablo (former), Light (former), Lime (deceased), Voltaic (deceased), Yo-Yo (deceased), Black Spider (traitor), Deathstroke (traitor)

DEADLY DISAGREEMENTS

Keeping the Squad in line during missions often proves difficult. The Joker's Daughter and Harley Quinn don't see eye to eye and Deathstroke betrayed the team to the Russians.

Task Force X is a secret team, run by Amanda Waller for the US government. Made up of convicted criminals in super-villain costumes, the task force cannot be linked to the government. The roster constantly changes, as different criminals are chosen for their particular sets of skills. The team's nickname — Suicide Squad — reflects the deadly nature of its missions.

"I want to use prisoners with nothing to lose and everything to gain."

The Squad is kept in line by explosives implanted at the base of their necks. If they try to escape or change the mission, Waller can detonate them.

DEADSHOT

VITAL STATS

Real Name: Floyd Lawton
Occupation: Mercenary
Height: 1.85 m
Weight: 87.5 kg
Base: Belle Reve Penitentiary
Allies: Suicide Squad, Amanda Waller, Harley Quinn
Foes: Batman, Deathstroke

POWERS AND ABILITIES

One of the best marksmen on the planet; armed with wrist cannons and an eye sight in his mask; wears armoured suit; adept at using nearly all types of firearms; efficient hand-to-hand combatant; eyesight can see various light spectrums.

FIRING SQUAD

As a member of the Suicide Squad, it seems as though Deadshot has found purpose in his life. He views some people – like his boss Amanda Waller – as a gun, and himself as a bullet, waiting to be fired.

Floyd Lawton was a poor boy growing up in the slums of Gotham City. One day, bullets from a nearby shooting came through the wall of his home and killed his family. That day, Lawton swore revenge and taught himself to shoot. He finally found and shot the men responsible, later finding employment with their boss as a sharpshooter.

Helmet protects against enemy fire

Loves guns, large and small

Eye sight synced with wrist guns

Carries weapons and plenty of ammunition

"I never miss."

133

DEATHSTROKE

VITAL STATS

Real Name: Slade Wilson
Occupation: Mercenary
Height: 1.93 m
Weight: 102 kg
Base: Mobile
Allies: Suicide Squad, Rose Wilson, Bronze Tiger, Team 7
Foes: Batman, Dick Grayson, the Teen Titans

POWERS AND ABILITIES

Highly trained hand-to-hand combatant; enhanced senses, speed, agility, endurance and strength; recently returned to a more youthful age; skilled in variety of weapons and firearms; brilliant strategist; connections in criminal underground, military and government agencies.

CLASHING WITH DEATH

A gun for hire, Deathstroke is billed as one of the world's best assassins. He has fought many fearsome opponents, from Batman and Harley Quinn to Wonder Woman and Lobo, managing to survive every fight.

Young Slade Wilson lied about his age in order to enlist in the army when he was only 16. He advanced quickly through the ranks, and soon joined the special ops group, Team 7. Slade was later the subject of a government experiment that made him into a super-soldier. He began life as an assassin and mercenary for hire: Deathstroke, the Terminator.

> *"Smiling? You like pain, Batman?"*

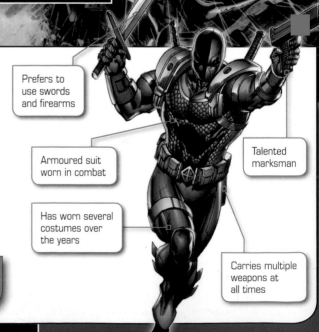

Prefers to use swords and firearms

Armoured suit worn in combat

Has worn several costumes over the years

Talented marksman

Carries multiple weapons at all times

CALENDAR MAN

VITAL STATS

Real Name: Julian Day
Occupation: Criminal
Height: 2.11 m
Weight: 131.5 kg
Base: Gotham City
Ally: The Squid
Foe: Batman

POWERS AND ABILITIES

Bulky and muscular; experienced brawler; obsessed with holidays, days of the week and the calendar.

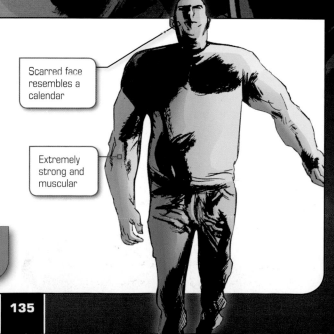

Scarred face resembles a calendar

Extremely strong and muscular

MARKING THE CALENDAR

When Batman met Aden Day, the boy was not being treated well. Batman donned his often-used criminal disguise as "Matches" Malone, and hit Julian Day's head against some tiles, creating a calendar-like scar on the villain's face.

Julian Day was a single father with a young son, Aden. In order to make ends meet, he took work as a hired thug for the crime boss known as the Squid. Julian was an excellent enforcer, but he was a terrible father. When Batman learnt that Aden was not being looked after well enough, he confronted Julian and placed Aden in a good home.

"Calendar...get... a...calendar..."

CATMAN

VITAL STATS

Real Name: Thomas Blake
Occupation: Bounty hunter
Height: 1.83 m
Weight: 81 kg
Base: Gotham City
Allies: The Secret Six
Foes: Batman, the Riddler

POWERS AND ABILITIES

Expert hand-to-hand combatant; feels oneness with big cats and is never harmed by them; handsome, with natural charisma and animal magnetism; extremely fit and agile; excellent senses; ferocious temperament.

FELINE SENSES

Once, Catman was simply minding his own business at a bar in New Mexico when he was kidnapped by the Riddler's men. Despite his captors telling him they worked for the Bureau of Alcohol, Tobacco and Firearms, Catman sniffed them out as imposters.

A bounty hunter who was kidnapped by the Riddler, Thomas Blake was held captive with only a pet kitten to keep him sane. After a year, he was set free until he was captured again, this time with five other criminals: the Riddler had a vendetta against the six for ruining the night of his marriage proposal. However, Blake and the others escaped, forming the Secret Six.

Catman befriended Secret Six member, Big Shot, not realising that Big Shot was Ralph Dibny, a man taking orders from the Six's enemy, the Riddler.

"We're not the good guys."

CAVALIER

VITAL STATS

Real Name: Mortimer Drake

Occupation: Criminal

Height: 1.85 m

Weight: 82.5 kg

Base: Gotham City

Allies: Arkham Asylum Inmates

Foes: Batman, the Batman Family, Batwoman

POWERS AND ABILITIES

Expert swordsman known to use electrified rapier; proficient with firearms; witty; adept strategist; costume armed with unexpected weapons; adept hand-to-hand combatant.

ESCAPE ARTIST

Despite being defeated by the Dark Knight on several occasions, Cavalier is quick to raise his rapier against Batman given the chance, participating in two recent Arkham Asylum breakouts.

An early foe of Batman's, Mortimer Drake adopted the name and mantle of the Cavalier after his love of antiques inspired him to rob museums for the finest collectibles known to man. Despite being confined to Arkham Asylum by Batman, Cavalier escaped during a breakout, but luckily, Batwoman was on hand to take the villain down yet again.

Smiles in the face of adversity

Often openly challenges Batman to a duel

Costume similar to those of the Three Musketeers

"Methinks a palpable and bloody hit —"

CRAZY QUILT

VITAL STATS

Real Name: Dr Paul Dekker

Occupation: Scientist

Height: 1.80 m

Weight: 78 kg

Base: Gotham City

Allies: Philip Kane, Dr Death, Hugo Strange, the Joker

Foe: Batman

POWERS AND ABILITIES

Unparalleled genius who created a way for cells to become new again; severely mentally unhinged; extremely knowledgeable in history; obsessed with the chemical compound Dionesium; carries and uses a firearm.

A STITCH IN CRIME

Paul Dekker was born in the Narrows to a poor family of artists who perished due to a broken gas pipe. A genius, Dekker invented an amazing medical process called "the healing stitch", but his mind later slipped into insanity.

When Bruce Wayne's uncle, Philip Kane, ran Wayne Enterprises, he hired the notorious Doctors Three: Dr Karl Helfern, who worked in bone; Professor Hugo Strange, neural matter expert; and Dr Paul Dekker, who worked in soft tissue. Like his partners, Dekker's life deteriorated, and he became an Arkham Asylum inmate after doing terrible things in order to meet Batman.

"Doesn't feel like a Batman story anymore, does it?"

Crazy Quilt used his incredible scientific skills to help the Joker develop a virus, which the Joker later released on Gotham City.

CLUEMASTER

VITAL STATS

Real Name: Arthur Brown

Occupation: Criminal, former game show host

Height: 1.80 m

Weight: 76.5 kg

Base: Gotham City

Allies: Lock-Up, Signalman, Firefly, Lincoln March

Foes: Spoiler, Batman, the Batman Family

POWERS AND ABILITIES

Clever strategist; trivia expert obsessed with clues; wears protective suit and hi-tech goggles; armed with weaponised capsules called plasti-pellets; connections to powerful figures in Gotham City underworld.

CLUELESS

Teaming with Lincoln March and several supposedly "D-list" villains, Cluemaster set out to rid Gotham City of Batman. Unfortunately, he didn't count on his own daughter, Spoiler, discovering one of his late night meetings with his accomplices.

The host of "Quizbowl", a trivia game show, Arthur Brown lost his job after yelling at a contestant. Upset that the "intellectually inferior" were wealthy while he was poor, he embarked on a life of crime as the Cluemaster. He attempted to prove his superiority over his robbery victims by leaving clues behind, clues that eventually led to his capture by Batman.

"I have taken everything from you, piece by piece."

Cluemaster used his ability to fly under the radar and plot the near-death of Batman, until he was seemingly killed by Lincoln March.

PARAGON

VITAL STATS

Real Name: Unknown
Occupation: Criminal cult leader
Height: 1.83 m
Weight: 88 kg
Base: Gotham City
Allies: Republic of Tomorrow
Foes: Dick Grayson, G.C.P.D.

POWERS AND ABILITIES

Expert at use of duel energy blades with rotating plasma core; leads cult of similarly armoured and weaponised extremists; genius-level intellect and thermodynamics expert; keen manipulator.

HERE TODAY, PARAGON TOMORROW

Nightwing discovered that Paragon had framed him for the murder of two of the Republic of Tomorrow's members. He confronted the villain and eventually turned him over to police custody.

Paragon is the leader of a fanatical cult known as the Republic of Tomorrow. As a teenager, he studied thermodynamics and was able to build a working reactor at just 16 years old. After developing a rotating plasma core to power energy blades, he adopted the name Paragon and began leading a group of armed cultists into what he viewed as a better tomorrow.

"The revolution, Nightwing... begins with your death!"

Wears armoured body suit

Enhanced sight through lenses

Paragon's symbol, worn by all followers

Designed energy blades himself

PRANKSTER

VITAL STATS

Real Name: Oswald Loomis
Occupation: Criminal
Height: 1.78 m
Weight: 77 kg
Base: Chicago
Ally: Cluemaster
Foes: Dick Grayson, Mayor Wallace Cole, Batman

POWERS AND ABILITIES

Genius-level computer hacker; master manipulator with dozens of followers; access to funds that allow for elaborate death traps; cunning, with a mind for revenge.

PULLING THE PRANK

When temporarily living in Chicago, Nightwing took on the Prankster and narrowly avoided dying in the villain's death traps. The Prankster was later defeated by Tony Zucco, the man who killed Nightwing's parents.

When Oswald Loomis was a boy, his father was killed on Halloween night — a crime for which the criminal William Cole was jailed. Loomis was wearing a Halloween mask that night, which he mailed to Cole, as a promise of revenge. He eventually got his payback when he framed William Cole's brother, Wallace, the mayor of Chicago, for embezzlement.

Loves to play cunning mind games

Mask similar to his childhood costume

"...where's the prank?"

AMYGDALA

VITAL STATS

Real Name: Aaron Helzinger

Occupation: Criminal

Height: 2.26 m

Weight: 155.5 kg

Base: Gotham City

Ally: Knightfall

Foes: Dick Grayson, Batman, Batgirl

POWERS AND ABILITIES

Near superhuman strength, endurance, speed and durability; almost mindless, with an uncontrollable berserker rage.

RIOT ON THE STREETS

Confused and easily disorientated, Amygdala was once hired by the villain Knightfall to cause havoc on Gotham City's streets alongside other villains including the Mad Hatter, Clayface and Mr Zsasz.

During the infamous Gotham City blackout, a mentally unstable behemoth of a man named Aaron Helzinger was undergoing brain surgery. Waking on the operating table — and lacking his brain's rage-controlling amygdala — he smashed his way out of the hospital and began to rampage through the streets. He chanced upon a young Dick Grayson and earned his nickname, Amygdala.

"...it hurtsssss!"

Grayson and his friends and performers at Haly's Circus escaped Amygdala's clutches, subduing the monster when he fell from a rooftop ledge.

THE RED HOOD GANG

VITAL STATS

Team Name: The Red Hood Gang

Base: Gotham City

Allies: Fellow Red Hood members

Foes: Batman, G.C.P.D., the Penguin, the Falcone Family

Members:
Red Hood One (possibly the Joker), the original Red Hood One (Liam Distal), Philip Kane, dozens of mysterious members

A PLAGUE ON GOTHAM CITY

The citizens of Gotham City lived in fear during the Red Hood Gang's reign of terror. The well-dressed thugs robbed banks, destroyed buildings, and made the city streets unsafe. Most people were too afraid to stand up to the violent gang — but not Bruce Wayne.

When Bruce Wayne returned home from training abroad, Gotham City was plagued by the Red Hood Gang. Led by the notorious Red Hood One, the gang was taking over some of the Falcone gang's territory. Before he adopted his identity as Batman, Bruce opposed the gang, only to have them destroy his operations base near Crime Alley, almost killing him in the process.

"Gotham's Finest!
Kill them all!"

After Bruce was injured by the Red Hood Gang, he realised he had to become more than a man to take them on — and so his Batman persona was born.

ANARKY

VITAL STATS

Real Name: Sam Young
Occupation: Criminal
anarchist
Height: 1.88 m
Weight: 97.5 kg
Base: Gotham City
Allies: Cult of followers
Foes: Batman, the Mad
Hatter, Harvey Bullock

POWERS AND ABILITIES

Natural leader and
extremely manipulative;
highly intelligent; commands
a cult-like army of devoted
followers; many connections
in the political world.

FOR THE PEOPLE?

Although he was later
proven a fraud by the
combined efforts of Batman
and Harvey Bullock, Anarky
managed to inspire many
people during his crusade,
including a young man
named Lonnie Machin.

When Anarky emerged in Gotham
City, he brought with him a revolution.
However, it was all smoke and mirrors.
When Sam Young was a child, his
sister was killed by the Mad Hatter.
Wanting revenge, Young adopted the
identity of Anarky and killed the
Hatter's old cohort under cover of the
fake rebellion. Batman stopped the
villain before he could kill the Hatter.

*"Shape your own future. The
Anarky revolution begins today."*

Anarky handed out thousands of masks based
on his sister's face, and encouraged Gotham
City's citizens to start their lives anew.

MIRROR

VITAL STATS

Real Name: Jonathan Mills

Occupation: Criminal, former federal agent

Height: 1.83 m

Weight: 93 kg

Base: Gotham City

Allies: Knightfall, Grotesque, Gretel

Foes: Batgirl, James Gordon

POWERS AND ABILITIES

Highly skilled fighter; extremely athletic; trained former federal agent; expert marksman; protective suit includes spiked knuckles and Utility Belt equipped with weapons and small gadgets.

TWISTED REFLECTION

Mirror keeps a list of individuals he believes should have died, and does his best to remedy that "oversight". One such name was James Gordon, before Batgirl interfered and saved her father's life.

Federal agent Jonathan Mills was the only survivor of a car crash that took the lives of his wife and twin daughters. He felt he had been fated to die, and decided to dedicate his life to killing others whom he believed should not have survived their near death experiences. After clashing with Batgirl, he later went to work for the criminal Knightfall.

"And you're not on the list."

Mirror was one of the first villains Batgirl fought after returning to life as a vigilante. So naturally, she was a bit nervous when facing him.

ARCHITECT

VITAL STATS

Real Name: Dillon May

Occupation: Criminal

Height: 1.83 m

Weight: 89 kg

Base: Gotham City

Allies: Hush, Nicholas and Bradley Gates

Foes: Batman, the Batman Family

POWERS AND ABILITIES

Modified construction suit grants him durability, speed, enhanced strength and endurance; suit's limited oxygen supply allows for periods of underwater activity; mentally unbalanced with a serious vendetta against Gotham City's most powerful families.

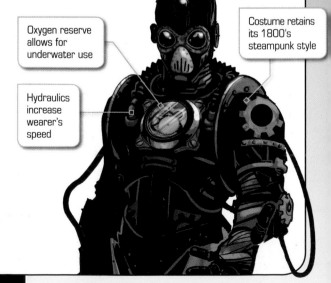

GATES OF GOTHAM CITY
When Dillon May adopted the suit of the Architect, he had no idea he was basing his vendetta on the words of a madman. Extended suit use leads to severe decompression sickness, and caused Dillon to lose his grip on reality.

In the late 1800s, Nicholas and Bradley Gates helped construct most of Gotham City's important buildings. Bradley made an underwater suit, but when he was murdered, Nicholas put on the suit to kill the likely culprit. Decades later, Gates's descendant, Dillon May, donned the suit, called himself the Architect and began destroying Gotham City's historical buildings.

Oxygen reserve allows for underwater use

Costume retains its 1800's steampunk style

Hydraulics increase wearer's speed

"...I wonder if you might come out and play?"

KILLER MOTH

VITAL STATS

Real Name: Drury Walker
Occupation: Criminal
Height: 1.88 m
Weight: 95 kg
Base: Mobile
Allies: Richard Dragon II, Red Dart, Brick, Count Vertigo
Foes: Batman, Green Arrow

POWERS AND ABILITIES

Uses hi-tech compression gun called a "stinger" to deliver highly concentrated air blasts; has many connections in the criminal underworld.

LIKE A MOTH TO A FLAME

Never one to pass up an opportunity, Killer Moth decided to work for a criminal calling himself Richard Dragon in Seattle. His mission was to take over the city and kill the hero Green Arrow in the process.

Years ago, during a terrifying superstorm that hit Gotham City, a woman called Moira Queen lent a hand during the crisis. Killer Moth, who was just starting his criminal career, decided to kidnap the wealthy woman. Unfortunately for the trigger-happy Killer Moth, Batman arrived to stop him, along with Moira's son, the fledgling Super Hero, Green Arrow.

Compression gun hooked to tanks

Wears gas mask to hide his identity

Calls his gun his "stinger"

"You're in Gotham now... everyone's a freak!"

147

BONE

VITAL STATS

Real Name: Louis Ferryman
Occupation: Criminal
Height: 1.88 m
Weight: 97.5 kg
Base: Gotham City
Allies: Tiger Shark, Dragos Ibanescu
Foes: Catwoman, Batman, Killer Croc

POWERS AND ABILITIES

Organised mid-level crime boss with connections in Gotham City's criminal underworld; holds grudges easily; often uses firearms; quite wealthy; employs criminals who wear white skull masks.

A BONE TO PICK

Catwoman first ran afoul of Bone when she stole from him. Enraged by her actions, he had his men destroy her flat and kill her business partner, Lola MacIntire. He has maintained a grudge against Catwoman ever since.

Louis Ferryman came from a poor family in Gotham City. He often moved, living at his parents' place, then his aunt's, then a group home. Bothered that fellow housemates would steal his things, Louis climbed the ranks of the criminal scene, taking pride in finally owning belongings. He adopted the name Bone and found true pleasure in owning jewellery, art and rare coins.

"Welcome, one 'n' all, to the great cat massacre."

Wears white suit and matching tie

Skin has texture and colour of human bone

Hires thugs to do his dirty work

DR PHOSPHORUS

VITAL STATS

Real Name: Alexander Sartorius

Occupation: Criminal, underground tribe leader

Height: 1.80 m

Weight: 76.5 kg

Base: Gotham City

Allies: Deacon Blackfire, Tinderbox

Foes: Batman, Catwoman, the Joker's Daughter

POWERS AND ABILITIES

Can shoot radioactive phosphorus flame at enemies; burns constantly with poisonous fumes; brilliant mind and natural leader; commands army of underground citizens.

RING OF FIRE

When clashing with Catwoman and the Joker's Daughter in the Gotham City underground, Dr Phosphorus revealed that his ultimate desire was to turn Gotham City into a giant volcano by causing explosions in the underground.

Catwoman first stumbled across Dr Phosphorus when she was searching for her friend Rat-Tail in the vast passageways under Gotham City. She passed into Charneltown, the area that Phosphorus ruled with his daughter, Tinderbox. Phosphorus revealed that he had been the victim of a nuclear accident and had fled to Charneltown so he could live somewhere hot.

> *"...I could flick my finger and fry you to a cinder."*

When Dr Phosphorus was imprisoned in Arkham Asylum, doctors summoned some of the country's top scientists to work out how to stop him from burning.

THE CREEPER

VITAL STATS

Real Name: Jack Ryder
Occupation: Criminal, former reporter
Height: 1.83 m
Weight: 88 kg
Base: Mobile
Ally: Killer Croc
Foes: Katana, Batman

POWERS AND ABILITIES

Hosts a mystical demon; superhuman strength, agility, endurance and durability; able to leap far distances; carries chains that he uses as weapons; can create manufactured tornadoes with his chains.

CREEPING THROUGH

The Oni Demon known as the Creeper came to our reality through a "crack in the world" during 16th century Japan. Twenty years later, he was discovered and imprisoned in the magical Soultaker sword.

Jack Ryder, a famous TV personality, was killed while reporting on a giant monster. Meanwhile, the Super Hero Katana was locked in battle with Killer Croc, who shattered her Soultaker sword, freeing a demon called the Creeper. These seemingly unrelated events converged when the Creeper took possession of Ryder's body, resurrecting Jack in the process.

"The Creeper rides again."

When Katana pieced her Soultaker sword back together, the Creeper became one of the main targets on her list.

DEACON BLACKFIRE

VITAL STATS

Full Name: Joseph Blackfire

Occupation: Criminal, cultist

Height: 1.91 m

Weight: 103.5 kg

Base: Gotham City

Allies: Professor Milo, Mr Bygone, the Joker's Daughter, Maxie Zeus, Dr Phosphorus

Foes: Batman, Batwing, Jim Corrigan

POWERS AND ABILITIES

Confident leader with natural charisma; uses violent techniques to gain followers; commands an army of devoted cultists.

BLACKFIRE AND BRIMSTONE

As an influential speaker, Blackfire gained a loyal army by finding people who had slipped through society's cracks. He lured them to his ranks by promising them all salvation under his rule.

Deacon Joseph Blackfire used to give sermons about the evils of Gotham City. Though he preached love, he was more interested in gaining power as the leader of his cult. He kidnapped Batman and used sleep deprivation and other violent methods to wear him down, but the Dark Knight escaped. Batman proved to everyone that the villain Blackfire was a fraud.

"My holy flock, our time grows near!"

Deacon Blackfire returned from the dead to plague Gotham City. He commanded an army of undead spirits, but was ultimately defeated by the Spectre.

FRIGHT

VITAL STATS

Real Name: Linda Friitawa

Occupation: Criminal, former geneticist

Height: 1.75 m

Weight: 65 kg

Base: Gotham City

Allies: Scarecrow, the Penguin

Foes: Batman, the Batman Family, Batwoman

POWERS AND ABILITIES

Can exhale nerve toxins; superhuman agility and strength; advanced medical knowledge; expert in genetics; adept hand-to-hand combatant.

FRIGHT NIGHT

Fright escaped Arkham Asylum during a mass breakout, but was soon imprisoned again. She was a useful source of information for Batwoman when the Super Hero was researching Batman and his methods.

A disgraced geneticist who lost her medical licence, Linda Friitawa began secretly experimenting on her boss, Dr Jonathan Crane — also known as Scarecrow. After transforming him into a Scarebeast, Friitawa adopted the name Fright and became a super-villain, spending her criminal career in and out of Arkham Asylum, taking advantage of the frequent breakouts.

"I can kill him with one breath, love!"

Linda Friitawa can exhale nerve toxins. In order to keep her powers in check, the guards at Arkham Asylum have to keep a breathing mask on her.

ANCHORESS

VITAL STATS

Real Name: Unknown

Occupation: Arkham Asylum inmate

Height: 1.57 m

Weight: 38 kg

Base: Gotham City

Allies: Dr Jeremiah Arkham, Dr Amadeus Arkham

Foes: Batman, the Joker's Daughter

POWERS AND ABILITIES

Has the ability to "quantum tunnel", or walk through walls; able to toy with the minds and memories of her victims; able to alter her own appearance.

BLAMING THE BAT

The Anchoress wrongly blames Batman for turning Arkham Asylum into a terrible place, rather than the peaceful asylum it used to be before the emergence of villains like the Joker and Mr Zsasz.

Born sometime before the 1900s, the woman who would become the Anchoress was interested in physics. When her parents tried to marry her off, a struggle ensued, ending with the Anchoress being knocked into a shelf full of chemicals. The resulting explosion killed her parents and gave her new abilities that enabled her to project her body's energy through various objects.

Appears helpless and frail

Can alter her appearance

Can enter one's mind with a touch

"They've all forgotten me here..."

153

REAPER

VITAL STATS

Real Name: Dr Benjamin Gruener

Occupation: Criminal

Height: 1.78 m

Weight: 75 kg

Base: Gotham City

Allies: Bane, Blackgate Penitentiary Inmates

Foes: Batman, the Falcone Family, Sumo, Firefly

POWERS AND ABILITIES

Wears armoured suit that strikes fear into those who encounter it; well-versed in medicine; adept hand-to-hand fighter; gauntlets contain sickle blades and firearms.

FLOWERS AT THE GRAVE

Batman recently battled the Reaper in the back of a floral truck with the help of Robin. The Reaper was attempting to send poisonous flowers to a wake for a member of the Falcone family.

Benjamin Gruener grew up in Germany during World War II, and was a survivor of the holocaust. He became a medical doctor, but his past made him fixate on revenge and he lost his sanity. As the Reaper, he has mysteriously cheated death to seek deadly justice for Gotham City's criminals, although he often clashes with the metropolis's true champion, the Batman.

"Now it's time to die."

After a riot in Blackgate Penitentiary instigated by Bane's forces, the Reaper joined Bane in a fight against the Arkham Asylum inmates.

BRUTALE

VITAL STATS

Real Name: Guillermo Barrera

Occupation: Criminal, enforcer

Height: 1.63 m

Weight: 66 kg

Base: Mobile

Allies: La Dama, Coyote, Rompe-Huesos

Foes: Dick Grayson, Blue Beetle, Brotherhood of Evil

POWERS AND ABILITIES

Expert with blade weapons, especially throwing knives; capable hand-to-hand combatant; extremely athletic and agile.

UNLUCKY SHOT

While quite formidable with his throwing knives, Brutale was actually instrumental in the creation of the Super Hero Blue Beetle. When one of his knives pierced the alien scarab Jaime Reyes was carrying at the time, the device was activated and turned Jaime into the Blue Beetle.

Hailing from Hasaragua, Guillermo Barrera was a deadly interrogator for his government's secret police, with a fondness for bladed weapons. When the regime changed, he set out into the world of freelance crime, as Brutale. After fighting Nightwing, Brutale worked for crime boss La Dama in El Paso, Texas, where he fought Blue Beetle and lost.

"— the little hero won't get far with a blade in his spine."

Brutale's costume is covered with throwing knives. While they might appear ornamental, Brutale can and will use every blade at his disposal.

DR SIMON HURT

VITAL STATS

Real Name: Dr Thomas
Wayne
Occupation: Criminal
Height: 1.83 m
Weight: 93 kg
Base: Gotham City
Allies: The Club of Villains,
the Black Glove
Foes: Batman, Robin

POWERS AND ABILITIES

Master manipulator and
plotter; does not age;
extremely smart; very
wealthy, with connections in
high society, the worldwide
underworld, the supernatural
world and various secret
societies; capable hand-to-
hand combatant.

ALLEGED ALLEGIANCE

Dr Hurt wanted to defeat Batman,
and saw Robin as a useful pawn
in his game. He offered to spare
Robin's life if he swore to be his
partner. But Robin already had a
teammate, and he and Batman
soon showed the doctor the
true meaning of "Hurt".

While he is indeed Dr Thomas Wayne,
Dr Hurt is not Bruce Wayne's father,
but an ancestor who cheated death by
releasing a devil called Barbatos back
in 1765. Centuries later, Hurt met
Batman and planted seeds of defeat
in his mind by posing as a psychologist
early in the Dark Knight's career.
Hurt later triggered Batman's mental
breakdown in an attempt to kill the hero.

> *"...the Dark Knight is dead. Here's
> to crime. And the Black Glove."*

With his own fail-safe programming buried
deep in his mind, Batman was able to
overcome Dr Hurt's mental manipulation.

THE CLUB OF VILLAINS

VITAL STATS

Team Name: The Club of Villains
Base: Gotham City
Allies: The Black Glove
Foes: Batman, the Batman Family, the Club of Heroes

Members: Dr Simon Hurt, Charlie Caligula, Scorpiana, El Sombrero, Le Dossu, Swagman, King Kraken, Pierrot Lunaire

THE CLUB SCENE

When Dr Hurt attacked Batman directly, the rest of the Club of Villains attacked Batman's allies. However, the Club of Heroes arrived in Gotham City to even the odds and give Batman time to triumph over the Black Glove.

Dr Hurt waited decades to take over Gotham City, and had meanwhile formed many alliances with nefarious groups, including the Club of Villains. Created as the counterpart to Batman's allies in the Club of Heroes, the villains hailed from all over the globe. Many of them had clashed with Club of Heroes members, such as El Gaucho. The Club was a small part of Hurt's larger conspiracy, the Black Glove.

"Come, take your place for the danse macabre."

Batman gained a whole new Rogues Gallery when Dr Hurt assembled his Club of Villains, and many of the villains have gone on to challenge Batman, Inc.

DR DEATH

VITAL STATS

Real Name: Dr Karl Helfern
Occupation: Former scientist
Height: Varies with mutations
Weight: Varies with mutations
Base: Gotham City
Allies: The Riddler, Crazy Quilt, Dr Hugo Strange
Foes: Batman, Poison Ivy, James Gordon, Lucius Fox

POWERS AND ABILITIES
Superhuman strength, endurance and durability; armed with serum that causes rapid bone growth to the point of death; brilliant scientist; body constantly healing in strange new bone formations.

DEATH COMES KNOCKING
After becoming unstable and losing his job at Wayne Enterprises, Dr Death injected himself with an experimental bone-hardening formula, adopting a monstrous form. He used his new abilities to kill his former colleagues, under the Riddler's employ.

Years ago, during a citywide blackout, the police discovered a series of grotesque murder victims. The culprit was Dr Death, a mysterious man who earned his nickname by experimenting on animals in illegal labs. After looking into Dr Death's past, Batman battled the villain above Gotham City, a fight that Death seemingly didn't survive.

"I've been waiting so long to meet you, after all."

Brilliant mind bent on revenge

Serum causes elongated proportions

Teeth grown into disturbing fangs

JACKANAPES

VITAL STATS

Real Name: Jackanapes
Occupation: Criminal
Height: 2.21 m
Weight: 205.5 kg
Base: Gotham City
Ally: The Joker
Foes: Batman, the Batman Family

POWERS AND ABILITIES

Typical strength, stamina and endurance of a large gorilla; quick learner.

FUTURE THREAT

According to the Joker, Jackanapes was a fast learner and could even work on intricate machinery. If true, this intelligent gorilla could prove to be a major foe of Batman in the future.

One day, at Gotham County Zoo, the Joker spotted a baby gorilla playing with a stuffed monkey toy, similar to one he had as a child. The Joker kidnapped the gorilla and began to raise it as his own, training it in the ways of murder. However, Jackanapes seemingly died when he was knocked off a blimp during one of the Joker's elaborate crimes.

" ... "

Trained in operating firearms

Jester costume complements the Joker's

Armed with deadly weapons at all times

JAMES GORDON, JR

VITAL STATS

Full Name: James Gordon, Jr
Occupation: Criminal
Height: 1.78 m
Weight: 72 kg
Base: Gotham City
Allies: Knightfall, Suicide Squad
Foes: Batgirl, James Gordon, Barbara Kean Gordon

POWERS AND ABILITIES

Psychotic master plotter and manipulator; many underworld connections; extremely intelligent; expert at covering up his crimes; aware of Batgirl's double life.

KILLER INSTINCT

When James Gordon, Jr reemerged in Batgirl's life, he played twisted games with his sister, even attempting to kill their mother, Barbara Kean Gordon. During one dramatic fight, Batgirl defeated James, mistakenly believing she'd killed him.

As a baby, James Gordon, Jr never cried, and as he got older, his family could sense coldness behind his eyes. When James killed the family cat and threatened the same violence to his sister Barbara, his mother left, abandoning Barbara in the process. Barbara grew up to become Batgirl, while James grew up to be every bit as evil as his family knew him to be.

"You. Will. Never. Be free of me."

James knows Barbara Gordon well enough to manipulate her. He even let Batgirl believe he was dead while he served as a Suicide Squad advisor.

BLACK MASK

VITAL STATS

Real Name: Roman Sionis
Occupation: Criminal
Height: 1.85 m
Weight: 88.5 kg
Base: Gotham City
Allies: The False Face Society
Foes: Batman, the Mad Hatter

POWERS AND ABILITIES

Wears ebony mask that seems to give him telepathic and telekinetic powers; natural leader; expert strategist; capable hand-to-hand combatant; very intelligent; expert in torture techniques.

MASK VS HAT

Black Mask's father's casket has long been one of the holy grails for the Mad Hatter, another of Batman's foes obsessed with mind control. This put the Hatter and Black Mask at odds, and made them natural rivals.

The rich yet disturbed heir to the Janus Cosmetics company, Roman Sionis was rumoured to have played an active part in his parents' death when their home burned to the ground. Obsessed with masks, Roman carved his infamous black mask out of his father's coffin, later discovering that the casket was made of a strange material that gave him special abilities.

"Can't you see your mind is too weak to defend against my probe?!"

Uses mask to control False Face Society

Accustomed to wearing expensive clothes

Fancy suit juxtaposed with frightful mask terrifies foes

BLACK SPIDER

VITAL STATS

Real Name: Eric Needham
Occupation: Vigilante
Height: 1.78 m
Weight: 78.5 kg
Base: Gotham City
Ally: Basilisk
Foes: Batman, Suicide Squad, Amanda Waller

POWERS AND ABILITIES

Master martial artist; wears armoured suit equipped with a variety of weapons and devices; weapons expert who often uses kamas; excellent athlete and gymnast; strong desire to seek vengeance against all criminals.

EYE OF THE SPIDER

Black Spider's mask is equipped with special lenses that allow him to utilise thermal imaging and get a better read on his target, even in a room that's pitch black or obscured by smoke.

When government agent Amanda Waller proposed the idea of the Suicide Squad, a task force of super-villains that offered her complete deniability, Black Spider was a top choice on her list of recruits. An old enemy of Batman, Black Spider was a Gotham City vigilante whose violent methods proved too extreme for the Dark Knight.

"I'm not done here yet."

While on the Suicide Squad, Black Spider proved he was as corrupt as ever when he betrayed the team to the terrorist organisation called Basilisk.

MAXIE ZEUS

VITAL STATS

Full Name: Maximilian Zeus

Occupation: Criminal

Height: 1.68 m

Weight: 61 kg

Base: Gotham City

Allies: Deacon Blackfire, Professor Milo, the Joker's Daughter

Foes: Batman, Batwing, the Batman Family

POWERS AND ABILITIES

Fit and athletic; capable hand-to-hand combatant; intelligent natural leader with a severe god complex; many connections in the business world and the criminal underworld.

THE POWER OF ZEUS

While staying in Arkham Asylum, Maxie Zeus was rendered near catatonic and felt nothing. This made him especially difficult to best in a fight, as the hero Batwing soon discovered firsthand.

For a time, **Maxie Zeus** was a successful crime boss in Gotham City. However, he began to lose his grip on reality and think of himself as a god, despite being bested by his enemy, the Batman. Later sentenced to a stay in Arkham Asylum, Zeus briefly hosted the spirit of Deacon Blackfire in his own body. This led to a battle with Batwing and the Spectre.

Zeus was treated like the god he believed he was when he joined a cult intent on resurrecting Deacon Blackfire, whose spirit possessed his body.

"**Bow down *to me*, mortal.**"

EMPEROR BLACKGATE

VITAL STATS

Real Name: Ignatius Ogilvy

Occupation: Criminal

Height: 1.91 m

Weight: 102 kg

Base: Gotham City

Allies: Poison Ivy,
Mr Mosaic, Hypnotic,
Imperceptible Man,
Mr Zsasz

Foes: Batman, the Penguin,
the Batman Family

POWERS AND ABILITIES

Brilliant strategist who
quickly climbed the criminal
ranks; superhuman
strength and durability
from serum partially
created by Poison Ivy.

KING OF THE MOUNTAIN

After powering himself
up with a combination
of Man-Bat serum,
Venom and a plant-
based formula,
Emperor Penguin was
arrested and taken to
jail. There he quickly
became the so-called
king of the prison,
changing his moniker
to Emperor Blackgate.

Unafraid to steal
the Penguin's
fashion and title

Master
manipulator
with high IQ

Powerful
connections in
the underworld

Ignatius Ogilvy rose to power as the
Penguin's right hand man. But when
the Joker forced the Penguin to help
him in his latest scheme, Ogilvy
claimed the Penguin's empire for
his own as Emperor Penguin. He
injected himself with a secret formula
to become a physical threat, but was
ultimately defeated by Batman and
incarcerated in Blackgate Penitentiary.

*"The dawn of a new era...and the
empire of Emperor Penguin."*

FIREBUG

VITAL STATS

Real Name: Unknown
Occupation: Criminal, arsonist
Height: 1.75 m
Weight: 81.5 kg
Base: Gotham City
Allies: Various employers
Foes: Batgirl, Batman

POWERS AND ABILITIES

Uses military grade fast burning accelerant to start and spread fires; wears protective fireproof armour; employs rocket launchers and incendiary grenades; single-minded focus on his mission once hired.

SOLDIER OF FORTUNE?

Little is known about Firebug's past, but the medals he wears on his otherwise unadorned suit imply a military background. He is obviously highly skilled, and shows no signs of guilt or remorse for his actions.

While probably not as well known as the similar Gotham City villain, Firefly, Firebug doesn't let the competition get to him. As a freelance arsonist, Firebug takes his jobs seriously, recently clashing with Batgirl when she was tracking down accomplices of the Joker. Killing police officers at the behest of his employer, Firebug was eventually defeated by the determined Batgirl.

"You shouldn't have come here to mess with Firebug, girl!"

Firebug's suit seems more utilitarian than those of most costumed criminals. A consummate professional, he prides himself on his work.

FIREFLY

VITAL STATS

Real Name: Ted Carson
Occupation: Criminal
Height: 1.80 m
Weight: 76 kg
Base: Gotham City
Allies: Cluemaster,
Lock-Up, Signalman
Foes: Batman, Dick
Grayson, Batgirl,
the Batman Family

POWERS AND ABILITIES

Uses stolen Firefly suit
that is capable of flight and
protects wearer from heat
and other damage; suit
can fire blasts of flame;
equipped with flame sword
and incendiary grenades.

FLY VS FLY

Ted Carson stole technology and
the name Firefly from Garfield
Lynns, a talented, yet easily
angered pyrotechnics expert.
His advanced Firefly suit can
fly with the use of fiery wings.

Movie star Cindy Cooke had lots of
adoring and obsessive fans. So when
her talent agency, production company
and the home of her ex-boyfriend, Ted
Carson, burned down, there were plenty
of suspects. It took the combined
efforts of Nightwing and Batgirl to
discover that Carson himself was the
Firefly, having faked his own death in
order to live a private life with Cindy.

*"I'm sorry...but
this is personal."*

As Firefly, Carson attempted to frame the
deceased Garfield Lynns for his crimes, but all his
attacks were merely an elaborate smokescreen.

GENTLEMAN GHOST

VITAL STATS

Real Name: Jim Craddock
Occupation: Criminal
Height: 1.80 m
Weight: 80 kg
Base: Gotham City
Allies: The undead
Foes: Batman, Batwing,
Midnight Shift, Hawkman

POWERS AND ABILITIES

Ghost-like, with the ability
to phase through objects
at will; naturally charming;
highly intelligent; a master
plotter; can project bug-like
appendages from his body
to aid in fighting; able to
alter his flesh to appear
invisible or like that of a
horrible monster; can be
driven away by Nth metal.

TO THE NTH DEGREE

Despite his sometimes
monstrous appearance, the
Gentleman Ghost can often
charm those that cross his
path. One surefire way to
keep him at bay, however,
is by using the Thanagarian
element, Nth metal.

Although his story remains unconfirmed,
due to his tendency to fabricate a tale
or two, the super-villain calling himself
the Gentleman Ghost claims to not
be a ghost at all. Hundreds of years
ago, Jim Craddock was cursed by a
witch who made him do her thievery.
After her death, the Gentleman Ghost
continued his criminal career, clashing
with Hawkman and later, Batman.

*"Take it from me...dead
lasts a very long time!"*

Hawkman first crossed paths with the Gentleman
Ghost when the Ghost was searching for an
artefact that could vanquish armies of the dead.

FLAMINGO

VITAL STATS

Full Name: Eduardo Flamingo

Occupation: Enforcer, assassin

Height: 1.91 m

Weight: 90 kg

Base: Gotham City

Allies: Hush, Penitente Cartel

Foes: Batman, Red Hood, the Batman Family

POWERS AND ABILITIES

Expert hand-to-hand combatant; weapons expert, particularly skilled in use of whips, swords and firearms; feared throughout the criminal underworld; expert motorcycle driver; lobotomised and unpredictable.

PRETTY HORRIFIC IN PINK

The Flamingo's colourful uniform and flair for pizazz hide the truly lethal skills of this masked murderer. He more often than not can be found atop his pink motorcycle, using his whip with deadly results.

The killer named Flamingo had created quite a reputation for himself before he arrived in Gotham City to challenge Batman and Robin. As an alpha-enforcer for the greedy Penitente Cartel, he was known for showing no mercy. Attracted to Gotham City by the actions of the Red Hood, Flamingo fought Dick Grayson, who only defeated him with the Red Hood's help.

"Heh Heh Heh."

The Flamingo once challenged Batman in his Batmobile, but the Batmobile trumps a motorcycle in any fight. Batman easily took the villain down.

LARK

VITAL STATS

Real Name: Unknown
Occupation: Criminal
Height: 1.70 m
Weight: 60 kg
Base: Gotham City
Ally: The Penguin
Foes: Batman, the Batman Family

POWERS AND ABILITIES

Excellent hand-to-hand combatant; adept with firearms; cool under pressure; access to the Penguin's impressive information network.

BIRDS OF A FEATHER

Aside from serving as the Penguin's chauffeur and bodyguard, Lark is also the villain's sounding board. She is privy to information others in his organisation are not, and is often an accomplice to his horrendous crimes.

As a general rule, the Penguin likes to surround himself with beautiful women to serve as bodyguards. While some of his employees, like Black Canary and Starling, didn't quite work out, others have stayed by his side through thick and thin, such as Lark. She is often tasked with keeping a watchful eye over the Penguin while aboard his floating Iceberg Casino.

"Your wish is our command, Mr Penguin."

Wears earpiece to keep informed

Always ready for a fight

Normally dressed all in black

Carries handgun on person at all times

GREAT WHITE SHARK

VITAL STATS

Real Name: Warren White
Occupation: Criminal
Height: 1.80 m
Weight: 84 kg
Base: Gotham City
Allies: Humpty Dumpty, Tally Man
Foes: Batman, the Batman Family

POWERS AND ABILITIES

Adept hand-to-hand combatant; keeps himself in top physical condition; has teeth filed to sharp points; brilliant strategist and schemer; has no moral compass.

SHARK ATTACK

Despite being held at Arkham Asylum, the Great White Shark has managed to run a powerful criminal empire from behind bars. He is a far cry from the "new fish" who was terrified to even enter the asylum a while ago.

Called "the Great White Shark" by the press, Warren White perpetrated one of the greatest acts of financial fraud in history. But instead of doing hard time, White pled insanity. The judge was not deceived and sent him to Arkham Asylum where White truly began to resemble his nickname when he lost his nose and ears while trapped in Mr Freeze's refrigerated cell.

"Who's the new fish?"

Great White Shark wasted no time in leaping into the fray during a recent battle between Arkham's inmates and those of Blackgate Penitentiary.

PROFESSOR MILO

VITAL STATS

Real Name: Achilles Milo
Occupation: Criminal, former professor at Gotham Academy
Height: 1.83 m
Weight: 72.5 kg
Base: Gotham City
Allies: Deacon Blackfire, the Joker's Daughter, Maxie Zeus
Foes: Batman, the Batman Family

POWERS AND ABILITIES

Expert in chemistry with a genius-level IQ; expert plotter and manipulator; many connections in the criminal underworld.

RUNNING MAN

After his latest scheme at Arkham was foiled by the intervention of the supernatural hero called the Spectre, Professor Milo tried to flee the country but was stopped by the Batman and his newest Batplane.

Often using his expertise to obtain positions of authority, Professor Milo is a talented chemist who has put his knowledge to evil ends many times. Most recently, Milo posed as a doctor at Arkham Asylum, sneaking patients into underground chambers for cult leader Deacon Blackfire. He was also a teacher at Gotham Academy until his corruption became apparent.

"...this man is suffering. He wants us to help him."

When allied with the cultist Deacon Blackfire, Milo used his knowledge of chemistry to drug Blackfire's recruits, forcing them to obey him.

HUMPTY DUMPTY

VITAL STATS

Real Name: Humphry Dumpler

Occupation: Criminal

Height: 1.91 m

Weight: 158 kg

Base: Gotham City

Ally: Great White Shark

Foes: Batman, Batgirl, the Batman Family

POWERS AND ABILITIES

Disturbed mind with a penchant for breaking things and trying to put them back together again; appears to have the intellect of a child; has a large body with substantial strength.

ALL FALL DOWN

Humpty Dumpty almost single-handedly changed the face of Gotham City by inadvertently destroying many of the large over-the-top props that formerly graced the town's famous skyline.

Humphry Dumpler's life fell apart after his home was destroyed by a misplaced wrecking ball. He soon became obsessed with taking things apart and putting them back again, including trains and traffic lights. Dubbed Humpty Dumpty, the unbalanced Dumpler caused an untold number of injuries due to the fact that he couldn't quite repair the damage he created.

"Snips and snails and puppy dog tails."

Often a resident at Arkham Asylum, Humpty Dumpty is not very popular — since he sometimes likes to "fix" people he views as broken.

HYPNOTIC

VITAL STATS

Real Name: Unknown

Occupation: Criminal

Height: 1.83 m

Weight: 89 kg

Base: Gotham City

Allies: The Penguin, Mr Combustible, Mr Toxic, Imperceptible Man, Mr Mosaic, Emperor Blackgate

Foes: Batman, the Batman Family, the Falcone Family

POWERS AND ABILITIES

Highly intelligent; utilises radio control waves to take over the minds of his victims; maintains powerful connections in the criminal underworld.

THE EYES HAVE IT

Hypnotic saw himself facing action in Gotham City sooner than expected when he battled Batman while aboard the Penguin's Iceberg Casino. He quickly discovered his hypnotic abilities had no effect on the Dark Knight.

Hypnotic made his debut in Gotham City along with several other new players who were organised and mentored by the Penguin. As part of his mentorship, Hypnotic was forced to pay part of his earnings to the Penguin. So when the Penguin's empire was briefly taken over by Emperor Blackgate, Hypnotic had no qualms about switching allegiances.

Highly intelligent crime boss

Uses radio waves to control minds

Shows little loyalty to anyone

"Stand back. I'll take control —"

IMPERCEPTIBLE MAN

VITAL STATS

Real Name: Unknown
Occupation: Criminal
Height: Unknown
Weight: Unknown
Base: Gotham City
Allies: The Penguin, Mr Toxic, Mr Combustible, Hypnotic, Mr Mosaic, Emperor Blackgate
Foes: Batman, the Batman Family, the Falcone Family

POWERS AND ABILITIES

Is completely invisible except for the clothes he chooses to wear; highly intelligent; many useful connections in the criminal underworld.

MARCHING ORDERS

Having previously worked for the Penguin, the Imperceptible Man and a few of his fellow criminals were called to a meeting by their temporary boss Ignatius Ogilvy, the future Emperor Blackgate.

The Imperceptible Man is a mysterious criminal whose powers remain a mystery to the majority of Gotham City's citizens. An employee of the Penguin, the Imperceptible Man's work was interrupted by a brief stint of cooperation with the Penguin's replacement, Emperor Blackgate, before he and his allies returned to work for the Penguin.

Always wears glasses

Natural leader and crime boss, despite being invisible

Clothes do not turn invisible like his skin

Wore gas mask during the Man-Bat epidemic

"What are we going to do?"

BIG TOP

VITAL STATS

Real Name: Unknown
Occupation: Criminal
Height: 1.75 m
Weight: 257 kg
Base: Gotham City
Allies: Professor Pyg, Mr Toad, Le Cirque d'etrange
Foes: Dick Grayson, Robin, Batman

POWERS AND ABILITIES

Excess weight allows for nearly superhuman strength and endurance; excellent hand-to-hand combatant despite size; many connections in the criminal underworld.

THE BIG MYSTERY

So little is known about Big Top that there is some debate over whether the villain is male or female. Big Top insists upon wearing a tutu nearly all of the time, but has a fully-formed goatee.

Little is known about the super-villain Big Top. As a member of Le Cirque d'etrange, Big Top worked directly with Professor Pyg, and even stormed police headquarters to help fellow circus member, Mr Toad, escape custody. Unfortunately for Big Top, Batman and Robin were on hand to bring the criminals to justice.

"Didn't Toad tell you he had friends?"

Weight lends to powerful strikes

Strange appearance intimidates foes

Is quicker than appears

LOCK-UP

VITAL STATS

Real Name: Lyle Bolton

Occupation: Criminal

Height: 1.88 m

Weight: 109 kg

Base: Gotham City

Allies: Cluemaster, Firefly, Signalman

Foes: Batman, the Batman Family, Spoiler

POWERS AND ABILITIES

Expert knowledge of police procedure; extremely fit and athletic; adept hand-to-hand combatant; known to use police weapons including baton; employs hi-tech weapons as well, including an electrified net.

IF YOU CAN'T BEAT 'EM...

In a renewed effort to eliminate the threat of Batman for good, Lock-Up teamed with several minor super-villains under the leadership of Cluemaster. Lock-Up and his allies were hoping that their meetings would remain under the radar due to their D-list status.

Lock-Up is really Lyle Bolton, a former security guard with a thirst for his own brand of justice. Having tried and failed to become a police officer, Lock-Up has no regard for the legal system. He began kidnapping super-villains and locking them up in makeshift prisons. After the Dark Knight stopped Lock-Up's crusade, Bolton became just another villain in Batman's Rogues Gallery.

"It's true what they say... it's brutal at the top."

Maintains private vendetta against injustice

Wears attire similar to police riot gear

Extremely athletic and muscular

KNIGHTFALL

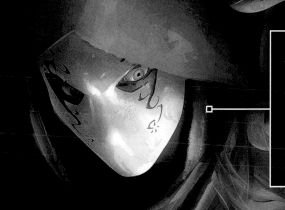

VITAL STATS

Real Name: Charise Carnes
Occupation: Philanthropist, criminal
Height: 1.80 m
Weight: 64 kg
Base: Gotham City
Allies: Mirror, Grotesque, Gretel, James Gordon, Jr
Foes: Batgirl, the Birds of Prey, Batwoman

POWERS AND ABILITIES

Expert manipulator and actor; extremely wealthy; adept martial artist with expertise in bladed weapons; severely mentally unhinged; connections in high society and in the criminal underworld.

KNIGHTFALL DESCENDING

While the public saw Charise Carnes as a philanthropist trying to help the neighbourhood of Cherry Hill, Batgirl discovered her cruelty early on. As Knightfall, Charise wanted to harm or kill every criminal in the city, no matter how minor his crime.

Raised by a wealthy property mogul, Charise Carnes was a teenager with a boyfriend named Trevor. But Charise was horrified when Trevor killed her family in front of her eyes. She didn't report her boyfriend, however, and was found guilty for his heinous acts. After a stint in Arkham Asylum, she reemerged as Knightfall, kidnapped Trevor, and made him pay for his crime.

> ## "We're going to change Gotham forever."

The villain made a later bid for Gotham City, with many of Batgirl's old enemies. But with help from other female heroes, Batgirl's side prevailed.

GROTESQUE

VITAL STATS

Real Name: Phillipe Rianne
Occupation: Criminal
Height: 1.80 m
Weight: 78.5 kg
Base: Gotham City
Allies: Knightfall,
Gretel, Mirror
Foes: The Birds of Prey,
Batgirl

POWERS AND ABILITIES

Superhuman strength
and endurance; mutation
allows for the ability
to absorb and release
electricity.

LIGHTNING STRIKES

When he first battled
Batgirl, Grotesque surprised
her by absorbing and
redirecting the electricity of
a nearby lamp. When they
battled for a second time,
he threatened to use the
electricity of a storm cloud,
but was shot by a henchman
with a change of heart.

Batgirl encountered the mysterious
super-villain called Grotesque when
he crashed a party for media mogul
Theodore Aiklin, demanding that Aiklin
hand over a valuable bottle of wine.
Aiklin refused, Grotesque escaped,
and Batgirl pursued him through the
sewers. He later ambushed her, but
was betrayed by one of his lackeys,
and Batgirl took the villain down.

Wears
gargoyle-like
mask

Mask once
shattered
by Batgirl

Channels
electricity
through club

Considers himself a
cultured individual

Dresses in
expensive
clothing

"What a lovely vintage she is."

GRETEL

VITAL STATS

Real Name: Lisly Bonner

Occupation: Criminal

Height: 1.78 m

Weight: 63.5 kg

Base: Gotham City

Allies: Knightfall, Grotesque, Mirror

Foes: Batgirl, Batman, the Birds of Prey

POWERS AND ABILITIES

Expert hand-to-hand combatant; inability to feel pain; able to control the minds of men and make them do her bidding; proficient with firearms and knives.

WORKING FOR CRUMBS

After failing to fulfil a contract to murder Bruce Wayne due to the intervention of Batgirl and Batman, Gretel later continued her life of crime working for Knightfall, another powerful adversary of Batgirl.

An aspiring journalist hoping to be the next Lois Lane, Lisly Bonner set her sights on a criminal, Boss Whittaker. When Whittaker found out she was wearing a voice recorder, he shot Lisly, and she plunged into the bay. The incident unlocked her mind-control powers, and she set out as the villain Gretel, intent on gaining control over the men that had made her powerless.

> *"I envy that. I'm green all over."*

Rendered bald from her injuries, Gretel now wears different wigs to match her mood. She faced Batgirl with green hair, and Batman wearing blue hair.

LORD DEATH MAN

VITAL STATS

Real Name: Unknown

Occupation: Criminal

Height: 1.80 m

Weight: 76 kg

Base: Mobile

Allies: Leviathan, variety of henchmen

Foes: Rā's al Ghūl, Batman Japan, Batman, Dr Darrk, Talon, the Outsiders

POWERS AND ABILITIES

Able to die and come back to life; mentally unstable; superhuman durability and endurance; capable hand-to-hand combatant; utterly fearless due to his particular condition.

SKELETONS IN THE CLOSET

After the fall of Leviathan, Rā's al Ghūl captured Lord Death Man in the hope of using the villain's death powers to his advantage. When Talon broke into one of al Ghūl's hideouts, he was forced to contend with the skeletal criminal.

A former opponent of Batman's, Lord Death Man reemerged recently in Japan when he killed the original Mr Unknown. On a Batman, Inc. mission, Batman and Catwoman stopped Lord Death Man with the help of Jiro Osamu, Mr Unknown's successor and the future Batman Japan. Unable to die, Lord Death Man has become a repeated thorn in Batman's side.

"Welcome to the Dead Heroes Club!"

Lord Death Man rarely takes life-and-death situations seriously, despite having clashed with Talon, the Outsiders, and even Batman and Robin in the past.

MARIONETTE

VITAL STATS

Real Name: Unknown, called "Mali"

Occupation: Criminal

Height: 1.75 m

Weight: 66.5 kg

Base: Chicago

Ally: Dick Grayson

Foes: Johnny Spade, the Mad Hatter

POWERS AND ABILITIES

Ability to mimic the movement and fighting techniques of others after witnessing them in action; extremely fit, fast and agile; excellent hand-to-hand combatant.

UNLIKELY ALLIES

Marionette is the Catwoman to Nightwing's Batman. Appearing to have a similar moral code, the two have worked together in the past. However, they still remain on opposite sides of the law.

The young Mali was once one of the Mad Hatter's favourite obsessions. Kidnapped and forced to do his mind-controlled bidding as his "Alice", she was shot by the Hatter. Cursed with a condition called "personality slipping", Mali relies on a rare drug, Kanium, to balance her mind. She does whatever she needs to, as Marionette, to keep a constant supply of the medicine.

The Mad Hatter's manipulation altered her mind

Unbalanced mind requires Kanium to function

Often steals to acquire Kanium

Skintight suit allows her range of movement

> "This *one wants to pull our* strings."

TWEEDLEDEE AND TWEEDLEDUM

VITAL STATS

Real Names: Deever and Dumfree Tweed
Occupation: Criminals
Height: Both 1.70 m
Weight: Both 85 kg
Base: Gotham City
Ally: The Mad Hatter
Foes: Batman, the Batman Family

POWERS AND ABILITIES

Capable hand-to-hand combatants; very intelligent; proficient in a variety of weapons.

DUMB AND DUMBER

More often than not, Tweedledee and Tweedledum serve as the insane villain Mad Hatter's hired muscle. Recently, they helped the Mad Hatter ransack homeless shelters in a frenzied search for the Hatter's delusional obsession, his lost "Alice".

The Mad Hatter is not the only villain to take his name from Lewis Carroll's book, *Through the Looking Glass*. When look-alike cousins, Deever and Dumfree Tweed, embarked on a life of crime, they adopted the identities of Tweedledee and Tweedledum. Having menaced Batman on their own, they have become allied with the Hatter.

"Don't worry boss. We gonna —"
"— crush the little man."

Very intelligent, despite acting otherwise

Share almost identical traits

Dress to match their fictional namesakes

Capable fighters despite their size

HERETIC

ROGUE

VITAL STATS

Real Name: None

Occupation: Terrorist

Height: 2.24 m

Weight: 156 kg

Base: Mobile

Allies: Talia al Ghūl, Leviathan

Foes: Batman, Robin, the Batman Family

POWERS AND ABILITIES

Superhuman strength, endurance and durability; weapons expert; master swordsman; excellent hand-to-hand combatant; seemingly unaffected by pain; wears protective armour that includes a jetpack to enable flight.

BORN TO KILL

The Heretic was meant to be Robin's replacement, one Talia made sure Damian was aware of before she cast him out of her family. The Heretic trained in Yemen and killed many superhumans in preparation for his role as Talia's ally.

Grown in a lab and hatched out of a whale carcass by Talia al Ghūl and her clandestine Leviathan organisation, the Heretic was a grotesquely aged "brother" to Talia's son, Damian Wayne — also known as Robin. Desperate to prove his love to Talia, the Heretic served her, destroying anyone who threatened Leviathan, including, eventually, Damian himself.

> *"I watch. I listen. I learn. I am Batman now."*

Underneath his robes, the Heretic wore Batman-styled armour. Despite his desire to please his mother, Talia hated the Heretic.

LADY VIC

VITAL STATS

Real Name: Lady Elaine Marsh-Morton

Occupation: Assassin

Height: 1.68 m

Weight: 54 kg

Base: England

Ally: Charlie Caligula

Foes: Batwing, Nightwing

POWERS AND ABILITIES

Expert assassin, martial artist, hand-to-hand combatant and sharp-shooter; prefers to use weapons that are old family heirlooms; well connected in the criminal underworld; quick, fit, agile and cunning.

LADY OF THE WORLD

Lady Vic seems at home in any environment, from the bright daytime streets of Mumbai, India, to the dark shadows of the Gotham City night. She is a professional, and usually does her job quickly and efficiently.

Lady Vic's name is short for "Lady Victim", but her actions point to her being more the predator than the prey. Hailing from a long line of British mercenaries, Lady Vic takes her job seriously. Recently, she nearly killed Batwing after taking on a mission to destroy any and all bat-themed vigilantes she encountered during her stay in Gotham City.

> *"You're not the hero.*
> *You're a paycheck."*

When Lady Vic first met Batwing, she easily bested the hero, despite his armoured suit of advanced technology.

MERRYMAKER

VITAL STATS

Real Name: Dr Byron Merideth

Occupation: Criminal, former psychiatrist

Height: 1.85 m

Weight: 88 kg

Base: Gotham City

Allies: Harley Quinn, Mr Freeze, Professor Pyg, Scarecrow

Foes: Batman, the Batman Family

POWERS AND ABILITIES

Behavioural modification expert, willing to utilise extreme and controversial methods; master manipulator; highly intelligent; access to Arkham Asylum patients.

IN LEAGUE WITH A MADMAN

The Merrymaker founded the League of Smiles, a gang devoted to the Joker. While he had no connection to the Clown Prince of Crime himself, he was more than willing to use the Joker's reputation for his own selfish gain.

A psychiatrist at Arkham Asylum, Dr Byron Merideth was one of the doctors assigned to evaluate the Joker. He then started up a private psychiatric practice to exploit those influenced by the Joker. Adopting the persona of the masked Merrymaker, he convinced his Joker-obsessed patients to do his bidding as soldiers for the Joker's "grand crusade".

"Merrymaker and the League of Smiles are just getting started."

The Merrymaker aided Scarecrow and a few other Arkham inmates in creating a mass hallucination in Gotham City known as Gothtopia.

MR TOXIC

VITAL STATS

Real Name: Hugh Marder
Occupation: Scientist, criminal
Height: 1.93 m
Weight: 109 kg
Base: Gotham City
Allies: The Penguin, Mr Combustible, Imperceptible Man, Professor Radium
Foes: Batman, the Batman Family

POWERS AND ABILITIES

Energy projection; excellent hand-to-hand combatant; genius-level intellect despite being mentally unbalanced; connections to Gotham City's criminal underworld.

TOXIC TOUCH

Batman once battled Mr Toxic in a laboratory inside Wayne Tower. The only way he could overcome Toxic's energy projections was by using a prototype energy deflector from his Utility Belt, developed by Lucius Fox.

Working on a way to travel forwards in time, scientist Hugh Marder ran into problems. Wanting to cure his own genetic disease, Marder began creating clones of himself that eventually deteriorated. Unable to stop his disease, Marder adopted the protective suit of Professor Radium, while his most stable clone became Mr Toxic.

Mind unbalanced after faulty experiment

Projects crackling energy

Helmet has been shattered by Batman

"I am no longer a carbon copy of you! I am your equal now, Marder!"

VORTEX

VITAL STATS

Real Name: Unknown

Occupation: Criminal, former quantum physicist

Height: 1.83 m

Weight: 92 kg

Base: Gotham City

Allies: Catwoman, Cheetah, Hellhound

Foes: Batman, the Batman Family, Killer Frost

POWERS AND ABILITIES

Force-based powers allow him to repel anything near his person; athletic build; need for revenge against his enemies.

BARS AND STRIPES

Vortex met Catwoman inside Arkham Asylum. To escape her cell, she convinced Vortex to stop taking his medicine and therefore activate his powers.

Vortex started out as a quantum physicist, working on an atom smasher. When he was sucked into the vortex of his own creation, he gained fantastic powers but lost some of his sanity. "Zebra man" found camaraderie among the criminal sect, and recently teamed up with Cheetah and several other animal-themed criminals including another Gotham City villain, Hellhound.

"Now I'm awake and I got some scores to settle."

Mentally unbalanced after accident

Force stripes cover entire body

Wears minimalistic costume

Powers can be held in check by medicine

MR COMBUSTIBLE

VITAL STATS

Real Name: Unknown
Occupation: Criminal
Height: 1.91 m
Weight: 90 kg
Base: Gotham City
Allies: The Penguin, Mr Toxic, Imperceptible Man, Hypnotic, Mr Mosaic
Foes: Batman, the Batman Family, the Falcone Family

POWERS AND ABILITIES

Seemingly made up of a mysterious chemical formula; can sense chemical compounds like explosives; very intelligent leader; many connections in the criminal underworld.

A SHINING JEWEL

Mr Combustible is highly resourceful and organised. This helped him rob several jewellery stores for Emperor Blackgate when a Man-Bat virus spread throughout Gotham City thanks to Blackgate's plotting.

While Mr Combustible's past remains a mystery, he seems a perfect fit as a Gotham City crime lord, with his strange looks and aristocratic personality. Forced to work for the Penguin when he arrived in the city, Mr Combustible has made the most of his situation by staying loyal to him, even during the brief time Emperor Blackgate took control of the Penguin's criminal empire.

"I'm sensing the presence of high explosives in this chamber!"

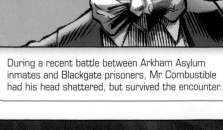

During a recent battle between Arkham Asylum inmates and Blackgate prisoners, Mr Combustible had his head shattered, but survived the encounter.

VENTRILOQUIST

VITAL STATS

Real Name: Shauna Belzer
Occupation: Criminal
Height: 1.80 m
Weight: 52 kg
Base: Gotham City
Allies: "Ferdie",
the Secret Six
Foes: Batman, Batgirl,
the Riddler

POWERS AND ABILITIES

Uses telekinetic abilities
to control the bodies
of others; connections
in the criminal
underworld; has a
dangerously disturbed
mind; manipulates
puppet to use as a
terrifying weapon.

SHARP AS A SPLINTER

Shauna customised a
puppet she stole from
a childhood entertainer,
placing drills in his palms
and treating "Ferdie" as if he
were alive. She often uses
Ferdie to attack her victims.

Appears
sickly
and frail

Telekinetic ability
makes her a top
ventriloquist

Her puppet
brings out
her dark side

Shauna Belzer was born with a twin
brother who stole the limelight. While
Shauna was dubbed "Shabby Shauna"
by schoolmates, her brother became
a child star. Discovering she had
telekinetic abilities, she used them to
punish her teasing classmates, and her
twin brother. As an adult, she began
a criminal career as the Ventriloquist,
naming her puppet after her brother.

*"I don't like it when people
are rude, Ferdie."*

WRATH

VITAL STATS

Real Name: E.D. Caldwell

Occupation: CEO of Caldwell Technologies, criminal

Height: 1.88 m

Weight: 95 kg

Base: Gotham City

Allies: Emperor Blackgate, Scorn

Foes: Batman, Alfred Pennyworth, G.C.P.D.

POWERS AND ABILITIES

Extremely intelligent; a wealthy businessman; access to cutting-edge weapons and vehicles; armoured suit equipped with variety of weapons; expert martial artist and hand-to-hand combatant.

DYSFUNCTIONAL DUO

Like Batman, Wrath considers himself a loner. But just as the Batman had adopted partners in the form of Robin and Batgirl, Wrath hired a cop killer in the form of Scorn. But when Scorn failed a mission, Wrath simply killed him.

The son of Mallory Caldwell, a man killed by the G.C.P.D., E.D. Caldwell went on to found Caldwell Technologies, a weapons manufacturer. Wanting vengeance for his father's death, he made a bid to purchase Wayne Enterprises, but Bruce Wayne rejected his offer. Caldwell nonetheless launched an assault on the G.C.P.D., stopped only by Batman's interference.

"...this is a game you're certain to lose."

Lenses enhance his vision

Highly armoured suit

Shock gloves can dispense 60,000 watts of current

VELVET TIGER

ROGUE

VITAL STATS

Real Name: Lani Gilbert

Occupation: Criminal, CEO of GilCom

Height: 1.65 m

Weight: 51 kg

Base: Mobile

Allies: Stolen tigers

Foes: Batgirl, Batwing

POWERS AND ABILITIES

Extremely fast and agile; has razor-sharp claws capable of cutting through cords easily; adept hand-to-hand combatant; computer expert; skilled in the use of knives.

EARNING HER STRIPES

When Batgirl first faced Velvet Tiger, she was taken by surprise by the villain's prowess in a fight. Velvet Tiger turned the tables on Batgirl, injecting the Super Hero with her own tranquiliser dart.

When a tiger attacked the office building of Luke Fox's new startup, FoxTek, Batgirl got involved, fighting off a second tiger attack at a similar company. Batgirl discovered this was the handiwork of a new villain in Gotham City, Velvet Tiger. Realising that this villain was Lani Gilbert, CEO of the failing tech company GilCom, Batgirl trailed Velvet Tiger, defeating her with the help of a remote-guided Batcycle.

> *"Better to live one year as a tiger, than a hundred as a sheep."*

Velvet Tiger picked the wrong fight by kidnapping Jo, a friend of Batgirl's. Batgirl fought hard to defeat the villain's tigers, allowing Jo to escape.

MORTICIAN

VITAL STATS

Real Name: Porter Vito

Occupation: Criminal

Height: 1.83 m

Weight: 80 kg

Base: Gotham City

Allies: The dead

Foes: Batman, the Batman Family

POWERS AND ABILITIES

Brilliant chemist; developed a formula to bring dead bodies to life; obsessed with stopping death.

WAKE THE DEAD

The Mortician was one of the many Batman villains who escaped Arkham Asylum during a recent breakout. He's not one to shy away from a good riot, and still holds a grudge against the Dark Knight.

After the death of his parents, the Mortician became obsessed with bringing the dead back to life. A gifted chemist who had been criticised by his parents for indulging in the sciences, he battled Batman after one of the "zombies" he created committed murder. After Batman defeated the Mortician's army of the undead, the villain used a serum to put his parents to rest once more.

"I often dream of killing him."

The Mortician was one of the inmates Maggie Sawyer and Batwoman interviewed when Batwoman was trying to defeat the Dark Knight.

TUSK

VITAL STATS

Real Name: Unknown
Occupation: Gang boss
Height: 2.49 m
Weight: 714 kg
Base: Gotham City
Allies: His criminal lackeys
Foes: Dick Grayson,
Batman, Robin

POWERS AND ABILITIES

Superhuman strength
and endurance;
extremely tough skin
that allows for
enhanced durability;
gang leader with many
connections in the
Gotham City underworld.

DE-TUSKED

While Tusk gained the upper hand
against Batman on their first encounter,
the villain ultimately lost the fight
thanks to Robin, who broke off one of
the criminal's tusks. Later, Damian
Wayne broke off the other tusk.

Little is known about Tusk's origins.
Batman began to concentrate on the
massive gangster's activities years
ago, when Dick Grayson was out
on his first official night of patrol as
Robin. Although Batman fired Robin
for not listening to his orders,
Robin attacked Tusk, and managed
to knock the villain from a helicopter,
earning his place by Batman's side.

*"Time to pick on
somebody my size."*

Why Tusk resembles an elephant remains
a mystery, but what is known is that he has
repeatedly returned to plague Dick Grayson.

NOBODY

VITAL STATS

Real Name: Morgan Ducard
Occupation: Mercenary
Height: 1.85 m
Weight: 97 kg
Base: Gotham City
Allies: Henri Ducard, NoBody II
Foes: Batman, Batman, Inc., Robin

POWERS AND ABILITIES

Highly trained martial artist and assassin; hi-tech weaponised armoured suit offers invisibility cloaking; enhanced vision; palm energy blasts; daughter currently wears similar suit with sonic upgrades.

GHOST FROM THE PAST

Batman first became aware of NoBody's campaign against him when the villain killed the Batman, Inc. agent known as the Batman of Moscow. NoBody's desire for revenge was strong — he blamed Batman for disgracing him in front of his father.

Daughter wears similar suit after Morgan's death

Special investigator Henri Ducard trained his son Morgan in the ways of manhunting, alongside Bruce Wayne — fostering a rivalry between Morgan and Bruce. Bruce later quit his training, and defeated Morgan as he tried to leave. Morgan returned as the villain NoBody, but was killed by Robin. His daughter, Maya Ducard, took on the role of NoBody.

Hi-tech invisibility capabilities

Armoured suit protects from damage

"...You know I'll be back to kill you all..."

TIGER SHARK

VITAL STATS

Real Name: Unknown
Occupation: Criminal
Height: 1.85 m
Weight: 92 kg
Base: Gotham City
Allies: Carmine Falcone, Bone
Foes: Dick Grayson, Batman, the Batman Family

POWERS AND ABILITIES

Adept hand-to-hand combatant; excellent leader; has many ties in the criminal underworld; drawn to endangered animals; uses a cane as a weapon as well as firearms.

THE FOOD CHAIN

When Carmine Falcone returned to Gotham City for a short period, Tiger Shark began working as his enforcer. Despite having an employer, Tiger Shark maintained a loyal entourage of lackeys who constantly spoke on his behalf.

A modern day pirate and smuggler, Tiger Shark made a major play to do business in Gotham City during the brief period when Dick Grayson took over for Bruce Wayne as Batman. Normally keeping just far enough off the coast of Gotham City to remain outside Coast Guard jurisdiction, Tiger Shark once used a gas pipeline to move materials in and out of the city.

"The tides will reclaim us."

Mask made of seal skin

Hieroglyphics tattooed on tongue

Prefers clothing made from endangered species

NOCTURNA

VITAL STATS

Real Name: Natalia Mitternacht

Occupation: Criminal

Height: 1.78 m

Weight: 63.5 kg

Base: Gotham City

Allies: Night-Thief, Wolf Spider, Morgaine le Fey

Foes: Batwoman, Maggie Sawyer, Batman, Killshot, the Unknowns

POWERS AND ABILITIES

Able to hypnotise others into believing a false reality or to be instantly smitten by her charms; connections to high society and the criminal world; adept at mind games.

WICKED WITCH

Nocturna once fought Batwoman when the evil sorceress Morgaine le Fey altered reality to appear like something out of a fantasy novel. Nocturna worked directly for le Fey until the Unknowns restored the world to its natural state.

Capable hand-to-hand combatant

Very intelligent and a master planner

Skilled fighter who keeps in shape

A former foe of Batman's, Nocturna first crossed Batwoman's path when a villain named Wolf Spider broke her out of Arkham Asylum. She later used her hypnotic skills to be legally freed from the institution. Meeting Kate Kane (Batwoman) soon after, Nocturna came close to becoming a hero — until Batwoman discovered her crooked ways and defeated her.

"Hello, Batwoman. Lovely to see you again."

TERMINUS

VITAL STATS

Real Name: Unknown
Occupation: Criminal
Height: 1.93 m
Weight: 109 kg
Base: Gotham City
Allies: Scallop, Bootface, Smush, Bathead
Foes: Batman, the Batman Family

POWERS AND ABILITIES

Employs a group of loyal lackeys who do his dirty work; vast stream of revenue enables purchase of warheads and technology to preserve his own life; armoured battle suit provides enhanced strength and endurance.

TERMINAL CASE

Terminus's rapidly deteriorating body required constant injections to sustain his life. He adopted a massive battle suit to fight Batman before his own death.

Battle suit armed with hi-tech weaponry

Body deteriorating at rapid pace

Technology helps to maintain life

Terminus's origins are mysterious. A villain whose body was literally falling apart, he knew the exact time of his upcoming death. Blaming Batman for his situation, he hired a team of criminals that had each been scarred by earlier encounters with Batman. They attacked Gotham City's citizens before Terminus unleashed a warhead — which was quickly defused by Batman.

"...I wanted to see you die inside a little, right before I do."

197

PROFESSOR PYG

VITAL STATS

Real Name: Lazlo Valentin

Occupation: Criminal

Height: 1.80 m

Weight: 120 kg

Base: Gotham City

Allies: Dr Hurt,
Le Cirque d'etrange

Foes: Batman, Dick Grayson,
Robin, Carmine Falcone

POWERS AND ABILITIES

Manic, unpredictable
behaviour; often aided by
henchmen and an army
of mind-altered Dollotrons;
capable hand-to-hand
combatant; considers
murder and violence
an art form.

THIS LITTLE PIGGY WENT TO GOTHAM CITY

After his laboratory,
located at Sinclair's
Meats in Old Gotham,
was burned down,
Professor Pyg sought
vengeance. He
retaliated against
his attacker, Carmine
Falcone, deciding
that all of Gotham
City would now
serve as his lab.

Recently
employed animal-
masked lackeys

Wears pig mask
at all times

When Batman first encountered the
villain calling himself Professor Pyg, it
wasn't Bruce Wayne wearing the cape
and cowl, it was Dick Grayson. In his
brief stint as Batman, Grayson teamed
with Robin to take down Pyg, a former
low-rent circus boss who decided to
become an underworld criminal.
The disturbed Pyg ran his operations
from a deserted amusement park.

*"Pyg will make
you perfect."*

KGBEAST

VITAL STATS

Real Name: Anatoli Knyazev
Occupation: Mercenary
Height: 1.91 m
Weight: 105 kg
Base: Russia
Allies: NKVDemon, Cheshire, Mayhem
Foes: Batman, Aquaman, the Others

POWERS AND ABILITIES

Expert assassin, hand-to-hand combatant, and acrobat; superhuman strength, endurance, and durability; adept spy with strong connections in the intelligence and criminal worlds; weapons expert; fully stocked Utility Belt.

MAKING MAYHEM

As a member of an organisation called Mayhem, KGBeast teamed with several other heavyweight mercenaries, including his apprentice, the NKVDemon. Their plot to take over the world was foiled by the Others.

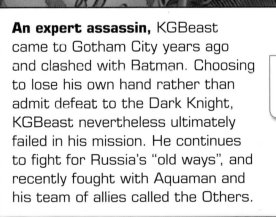

Wears mask to hide his scarred face

Protective suit bears Soviet Union colours

Turned his severed hand into a weapon

An expert assassin, KGBeast came to Gotham City years ago and clashed with Batman. Choosing to lose his own hand rather than admit defeat to the Dark Knight, KGBeast nevertheless ultimately failed in his mission. He continues to fight for Russia's "old ways", and recently fought with Aquaman and his team of allies called the Others.

"We shall restore our country to what it once was..."

RATCATCHER

VITAL STATS

Real Name: Otis Flannegan
Occupation: Criminal
Height: 1.78 m
Weight: 72.6 kg
Base: Gotham City
Allies: Cluemaster, Menace, Firefly, Signalman, Lock-Up
Foes: Batman, Batwing, the Batman Family

POWERS AND ABILITIES

Communicates with and controls rats; has connections to Gotham City's underground community and several above-ground criminals as well.

RAT FINK
Severely mentally unbalanced, the Ratcatcher keeps a live rat in his helmet. He often has conversations with his rodents, and uses them to spy on people on Gotham City's streets, essentially giving him eyes and ears everywhere.

A citizen of the underground, the vast network of cities and towns below Gotham City, the Ratcatcher is obsessed with other residents of that dark world: rats. Working with the villain Menace, he used his command over rodents to help kidnap Batwing's sister, Tiffany Fox. He later joined forces with Cluemaster in an attempt to destroy Batman for good.

"Heigh-ho the derry-o the cheese goes insane!"

The Ratcatcher has trouble speaking. He prefers to communicate with his rodent allies rather than the crime bosses he's worked with.

SUMO

VITAL STATS

Real Name: Unknown
Occupation: Criminal
Height: 1.96 m
Weight: 275 kg
Base: Gotham City
Allies: The Squid, Arkham Asylum inmates
Foes: Batman, Resurrection Man, Bane

POWERS AND ABILITIES

Extremely strong and heavy; quicker than his appearance implies; many connections in the criminal underworld; maintains impressive endurance and durability.

SUMO WRESTLING

Batman first met Sumo when tracing the source of a drug that killed Elena Aguila, a friend of Bruce Wayne's. Inside a shipping container, Batman activated a pair of red glow sticks, only to find himself facing Sumo's huge tiger tattoo.

A familiar face behind the bars at Arkham Asylum, Sumo cuts an intimidating figure in the criminal underworld. Batman first encountered the villain when he interrupted a smuggling ring Sumo had been running at Gotham City's docks. Batman triumphed over the enormous villain, learning that Sumo had worked with a Gotham City crime boss, the Squid.

Mentally unstable, he enjoys violence

Wears scant clothing and a sumo's mawashi

Enormous body can crush opponents

"I thought bats could see in the dark!"

RED ALICE

VITAL STATS

Real Name: Elizabeth Kane

Occupation: Vigilante, former criminal

Height: 1.80 m

Weight: 64 kg

Base: Mobile

Allies: Batwoman, the Unknowns

Foes: Mr Bones, Morgaine le Fey, Nocturna

POWERS AND ABILITIES

Skilled martial artist and gymnast; extensive understanding of military procedure; damaged mind from past trauma; adept hand-to-hand combatant; excellent marksman; wears protective suit equipped with variety of gadgets.

ALICE DOESN'T LIVE HERE ANYMORE

Red Alice and Batwoman are sisters, but they couldn't be more different. Red Alice is constantly struggling with her sanity, often quoting lines from Lewis Carroll's *Through the Looking Glass* as her own speech.

As a young girl, Beth Kane was kidnapped alongside her twin sister, Kate Kane, and their mother. While their father, Jacob Kane, managed to rescue Kate, Beth was presumed dead, only to reemerge as the very disturbed super-villain Red Alice. Fighting her own sister who had adopted the identity of Batwoman, Red Alice was eventually defeated by her Super Hero twin.

"Don't worry. I'm not here to kill you."

After surviving her battle with Batwoman, Red Alice straightened out her life to become a vigilante on the right side of the law.

THE SQUID

VITAL STATS

Real Name: Lawrence Loman
Occupation: Criminal
Height: 1.68 m
Weight: 78.5 kg
Base: Gotham City
Allies: Sumo, Calendar Man
Foes: Batman, Harvey Bullock

POWERS AND ABILITIES

Intelligent strategist and leader; many connections in the criminal underworld.

TANKED

The Squid had no qualms about making an example out of someone who had wronged him. When his own brother's crew stole from him, the Squid dropped one of the men into the tank of a deadly giant squid.

The Squid was a Gotham City crime boss who attracted Batman's attention after the death of Bruce Wayne's friend, Elena Aguila. Looking into Elena's death, Batman uncovered a network of criminals that included the Squid. Tracking him to an abandoned aquarium, Batman overcame the villain's pet squid before the Squid was killed by a rival criminal.

"...Gotham City is the monster that needs to be fed."

Comfortable, lightweight jacket

No costume needed to exude an air of danger

Not afraid to get his own hands dirty

INDEX

Main entries are in **bold**.

ARTIST ACKNOWLEDGEMENTS

Christian Alamy, Juan Albarran, Oclair Albert, Rafael Albuquerque, Laura Alfred, Michael Alfred, Marlo Alquiza, Brad Anderson, Marc Andreyko, Joy Ang, Ulises Arreola, Mahmud Asrar, Michael Atiyeh, Tony Aviña, Matt Banning, Al Barrionuevo, Eddy Barrows, Jacob Bear, David Beaty, Tony Bedard, Ed Benes, Mariah Benes, Bengal, Ryan Benjamin, Marguerite Bennet, Joe Bennett, Rain Beredo, Lee Bermejo, W. Haden Blackman, Fernando Blanco, Blond, Roger Bonet, James Bonny, Brett Booth, Geraldo Borges, Andrei Bressan, Vera Brosgol, Jimmy Broxton, Brian Buccellato, Cullen Bunn, Riccardo Burchielli, Chris Burnham, Jim Calafiore, Greg Capullo, Juan Castro, Keith Champagne, Howard Chaykin, Clio Chiang, ChrisCross, June Chung, Vicente Cifuentes, Scott Clark, Andy Clarke, Ronan Cliquet, Becky Cloonan, Andre Coelho, David Cole, Simon Coleby, Amanda Conner, Will Conrad, Darwyn Cooke, Paul Cornell, Jorge Corona, Jeromy Cox, Wes Craig, Andrew Dalhouse, Federico Dallacchio, Tony S. Daniel, Marc Deering, Tom DeFalco, Werther Dell'Edera, Jesse Delperdang, Tom Derenick, Johnny Desjardins, Dan DiDio, Andy Diggle, Rachel Dodson, Terry Dodson, Jed Dougherty, Christian Duce, Dale Eaglesham, Scott Eaton, Gabe Eltaeb, Nathan Eyring, Jason Fabok, Nathan Fairbairn, Romulo Fajardo, Jr, Ray Fawkes, Raul Fernandez, Eber Ferreira, Julio Ferreira, Juan Ferreyra, Pascal Ferry, David Finch, Meredith Finch, Brenden Fletcher, Sandu Florea, Fabrizio Florentino, Jorge Fornes, Gary Frank, Derek Fridolfs, Richard Friend, Lee Garbett, Alex Garner, Javier Garrón, Sterling Gates, Dave Geraci, Drew Geraci, Ransom Getty, Sunny Gho, Keith Giffen, Jonathan Glapion, Adam Glass, Patrick Gleeson, Joel Gomez, Julius Gopez, Mick Gray, Justin Gray, Dan Green, Michael Green, Ig Guara, R.M. Guera, Andres Guinaldo, Scott Hanna, Chad Hardin, Joe Harris, James Harvey, Jeremy Haun, Rob Haynes, Doug Hazlewood, Daniel Henriques, Scott Hepburn, Meghan Hetrick, Hi-Fi Design, Kyle Higgins, David Hine, Bryan Hitch, Sandra Hope, Corin Howell, Adam Hughes, Ken Hunt, Rob Hunter, Gregg Hurwitz, Frazer Irving, Mark Irwin, Jack Jadson, Al Jaffee, Mikel Janín, Georges Jeanty, Paul Jenkins, Jorge Jimenez, Jock, Geoff Johns, Staz Johnson, Mike Johnson, Henrik Jonsson, Ruy José, Juancho, Dan Jurgens, John Kalisz, Jon Katz, Karl Kerschi, Karl Kesel, Tom King, Tyler Kirkham, Scott Kolins, Ales Kot, Andrew Kreisberg, Andy Kubert, Szymon Kudranski, Michel Lacombe, José Ladrönn, David Lafuente, Serge Lapointe, Ken Lashley, John Layman, Jae Lee, Jim Lee, Jay Leisten, Jeff Lemire, Rick Leonardi, Yishan Li, Rob Liefeld, LLC, Scott Lobdell, Jeph Loeb, Alvaro Lopez, David Lopez, Emilio Lopez, Aaron Lopresti, Lee Loughridge, Jorge Lucas, Ant Lucia, Emanuela Lupacchino, Doug Mahnke, Marcelo Maiolo, Guy Major, Alex Maleev, Francis Manapul, Leandro Manco, Clay Mann, Guillem March, Alitha Martinez, Allen Martinez, Alvaro Martinez, Stefano Martino, Christy Marx, José Marzan, Jr, Jason Masters, J.P. Mayer, Dave McCaig, Ray McCarthy, Trevor McCarthy, Scott McDaniel, Mike McKone, Lan Medina, Hermann Mejia, Javier Mena, Jaime Mendoza, Jesús Merino, Jonboy Meyers, Danny Miki, Romano Molenaar, Jorge Molina, Sula Moon, Stephen Mooney, Tomeu Morey, Moritat, Grant Morrison, Paul Mounts, Dustin Nguyen, Tom Nguyen, Fabian Nicieza, Ann Nocenti, Mike Norton, Kevin Nowlan, Sonia Oback, Patrick Olliffe, Guillermo Ortego, Andy Owens, Agustin Padilla, Greg Pak, Jimmy Palmiotti, Dan Panosian, Eduardo Pansica, Pete Pantazis, Yanick Paquette, Jeff Parker, Sean Parsons, Fernando Pasarin, Allen Passalaqua, Jason Pearson, Paul Pelletier, Pere Perez, Cris Peter, Will Pfeifer, Javier Piña, FCO Plascencia, Francis Portela, Howard Porter, Eric Powell, Joe Prado, Jack Purcell, Joe Quinones, Wil Quintana, Frank Quitely, Khary Randolph, Norm Rapmund, John Rauch, Sal Regla, Ivan Reis, Rod Reis, Cliff Richards, Tom Richmond, Jeremy Roberts, Roger Robinson, Kenneth Rocafort, Robson Rocha, Prentis Rollins, Alex Ross, Stéphane Roux, Felix Ruiz, Matt Ryan, Sean Ryan, Juan Jose Ryp, Jesús Saíz, Edgar Salazar, Tim Sale, Daniel Sampere, Rafa Sandoval, Derlis Santacruz, Trevor Scott, Tim Seeley, Emanuel Simeoni, Gail Simone, Alex Sinclair, Paulo Siqueira, Dan Slott, Brett Smith, Scott Snyder, Ben Sokolowski, Ryan Sook, Andrea Sorrentino, Chris Sotomayor, Peter Steigerwald, Cameron Stewart, Jeff Stokely, RC Stoodios, Karl Story, Carrie Strachan, Mico Suayan, Goran Sudzuka, Duane Swierczynski, Ardian Syaf, Phillip Tan, Babs Tarr, Jordi Tarragona, Ben Templesmith, Art Thibert, Frank Tieri, Marcus To, Peter Tomasi, Andy Troy, James Tynion IV, Ethan Van Sciver, Roberto Viacava, Dexter Vines, Alessandro Vitti, Joe Weems, Scott Williams, J.H. Williams III, Judd Winick, Ryan Winn, Marv Wolfman, Walden Wong, Jason Wright, Annie Wu, Matt Yackey, Craig Yeung, Richard Zajac, Patrick Zircher.

SENIOR EDITOR Victoria Taylor
PROJECT EDITOR Shari Last
EDITOR Laura Nickoll
SENIOR DESIGNER Robert Perry
DESIGNERS Chris Gould, Pallavi Kapur
DTP DESIGNERS Umesh Singh Rawat, Rajdeep Singh
PRE-PRODUCTION PRODUCER Siu Yin Chan
PRE-PRODUCTION MANAGER Sunil Sharma
SENIOR PRODUCER Alex Bell
MANAGING EDITOR Sadie Smith
MANAGING ART EDITORS Ron Stobbart, Neha Ahuja
PUBLISHER Julie Ferris
ART DIRECTOR Lisa Lanzarini
PUBLISHING DIRECTOR Simon Beecroft

ADDITIONAL DESIGN Dynamo Limited

Dorling Kindersley would like to thank Josh Anderson and Amy Weingartner at Warner Bros. Global Publishing and Leah Tuttle at DC Entertainment. Thanks also to Julia March for the index, Joel Kempson, Lauren Nesworthy, Lisa Stock and Chitra Subramanyam for editorial assistance, and Lisa Robb, Radhika Banerjee and Ishita Chawla for design assistance.

First published in Great Britain in 2016 by
Dorling Kindersley Limited
80 Strand, London WC2R 0RL
A Penguin Random House Company

10 9 8 7 6 5 4 3 2 1
001–264931–Feb/16

Page design copyright © 2016 Dorling Kindersley Limited

A WORLD OF IDEAS:
SEE ALL THERE IS TO KNOW
www.dk.com
www.dccomics.com